REALSIMPLE
869 new uses for old things

edited by Rachel Hardage and Sharon Tanenbaum
photographs by James Wojcik / illustrations by Kate Francis
prop styling by Linden Elstran

REALSIMPLE Time
HOME ENTERTAINMENT

I WOULD NEVER SUGGEST that *Real Simple* has changed the course of human history, but we may have come close with New Uses for Old Things.

When someone begins to rhapsodize about why she loves *Real Simple*, invariably this section of the magazine is the first thing she mentions. Never mind that many people have trouble remembering what it's officially called.

"You know!" a loyal reader will exclaim. *"That section where you take things and turn them into something else!"*

Or: *"That repurposing…uh…clever ideas for another way to…oh, you know, that really smart article with so many great tips!"*

Or: *"That part of the magazine with all those surprising uses for household things!"*

And on and on. All expressed with fervor and wonder and joy. I now know it is possible to love something deeply and not know what it's called, which explains why it's perfectly OK for a parent to call her child by another child's name in a moment of stress or distraction.

In this age of reduce/reuse/recycle, New Uses for Old Things is the original green idea. Introduced in the monthly magazine in 2002, when our editors revealed how to use dental floss to neatly cut soft cheese, slice eggs, and even truss a chicken, New Uses for Old Things has served as a sort of beacon for staff members and readers alike. It has "smart," "surprising," and "good for the earth" all wrapped up into one. What more could you want?

And in case you're wondering whether it's easy to come up with those clever ideas month in and month out: It's not.

THIS YEAR, IN CELEBRATION of *Real Simple*'s 10th anniversary, we give you the book we've all been waiting for: the encyclopedic version of New Uses for Old Things, featuring innovative, who-knew? ideas for everything in your home, from accordion folders to zippered plastic bags. Never mind that you can't remember what the section is called. Really, it's the thought that counts.

Kristin van Ogtrop
Managing Editor, *Real Simple*

/ CONTENTS /

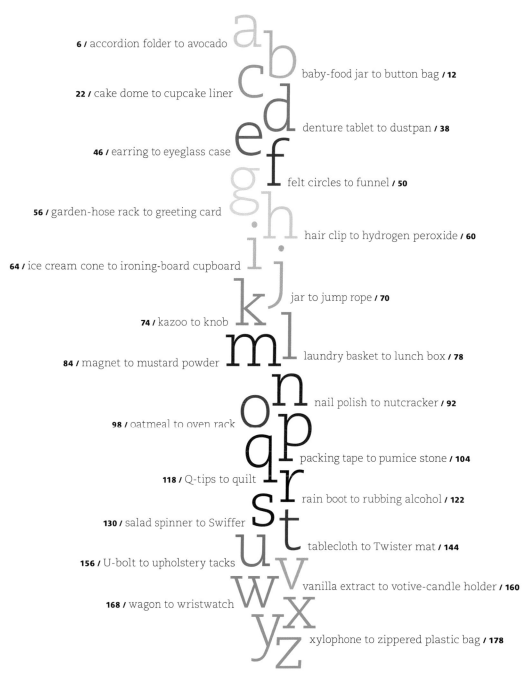

accordion folder to avocado ▶

accordion folder

USE TO: Be prepared for birthdays. Once a year, stock up on the perfect cards for all your family members and friends, plus a few all-purpose extras, and stash them in the slots, organized by month.

address label

USE TO: Ensure that all the books in your lending library find their way back home.
+ Avoid inadvertent gadget switcheroos. Label all the cell phones, cameras, and other look-alike devices in the house. Add your contact info and a Good Samaritan can return the phone you left on the plane.

aluminum foil

For this Master Multitasker's many uses, see page 10.

ankle weight

USE TO: Keep a top-heavy stroller from tipping. Strap a weight on each of its front legs.

antacid tablet ▶

USE TO: Lift bouquet residue from the inside of a vase. Add water and one tablet, let sit for a few minutes, swirl, and rinse.
+ Clean a toilet. Drop in two dissolving tablets, let the bubbles work for 20 minutes, then brush.

+ Soothe a bug bite. Dissolve two tablets in a glass of water, then dab on the solution.
+ Stage a science experiment for the kids. Fill a plastic film canister a third full with water, drop in a tablet, and replace the lid. Set it on the ground upside down and step back. The pressure will send the canister soaring.

apple

USE TO: Ripen tomatoes in half the time. Put them in a bowl with an apple and cover with plastic wrap.

apple cider vinegar

USE TO: Restore shine to dull hair. After shampooing and conditioning, rinse with two tablespoons of warmed vinegar to remove buildup. Hair will retain a faint scent.

apple container

USE TO: Store fragile holiday ornaments. The plastic cubbies will add a little protection to help those glass balls from your childhood make it through another year in one piece.

avocado

USE TO: Make a natural hair conditioner. Mash a ripe avocado and coat just-shampooed hair with the paste. Leave on for 15 minutes, then rinse thoroughly.

MASTER MULTITASKER / **ALUMINUM FOIL** / 1 Shield a muffin tin from burned-on batter drips by laying a foil sheet across it, snipping an X over each cup, and popping in liners. 2 **Lift stubborn wrinkles from a delicate silk, wool, or rayon garment by placing a foil sheet under it and passing an iron's steam three to four inches over the item several times.** 3 Twist foil into links to make a sparkly garland for a homemade party decoration (or a rainy-day distraction for the kids). 4 **Fashion a funnel of foil to neatly transfer salad dressings or condiments from tacky plastic bottles to pretty carafes or bowls (and back again).** 5 Slip a foil sheet between your stacked TV and DVD player to keep commingling electromagnetic fields from distorting the picture. 6 **Remove baked-on food from a glass pan or an oven rack by scrunching foil into a ball and scrubbing with dish soap in a circular motion.** 7 Protect doorknobs and hardware from splatters when you paint by wrapping them with foil.

baby-food jar to button bag ▶

baby-food jar ▶

USE TO: Simplify paint touch-ups. Pour a few ounces of new wall paint into a jar for when it's needed to cover the inevitable nail holes and scuffs.

+ Corral loose hardware for, say, furniture that has been disassembled for a move.

+ Design Rothko-esque Easter eggs. Fill a jar with dye, then dip half the egg in and let dry. Dip again, but only one-third of the egg. Repeat with both ends of the egg until you have stripes in varying widths and shades.

baby oil

USE TO: Refresh the shine of patent-leather shoes.

+ Remove latex paint from skin.

+ Slip a ring from a swollen finger.

+ Lift tar from feet after a beach day.

+ Restore shine to chrome, from faucets to hubcaps.

+ Untangle a necklace. Rub a few drops into each knot and gently work them free with a straight pin.

+ Make removing a bandage painless. Rub oil over and around the sticky parts before the big rip-off.

baby powder

USE TO: Prevent sweat stains on white shirts. Sprinkle powder on the underarms and the collar, then iron. The powder acts as a barrier.

+ Fake freshly washed hair. Sprinkle powder on, then comb through down to the roots.

baby spoon

USE TO: Serve dips or condiments at a party. Reuse those old shower gifts to spoon the sauce from a teacup or a candy dish for a presentation a tad more elegant than the squeeze bottle.

baby wipe

USE TO: Remove deodorant marks from a blouse. It takes just a few swipes of a wipe.

baking soda

For this Master Multitasker's many uses, see page 20.

banana

USE TO: Strengthen damaged hair. Mash a banana into a paste with a tablespoon of olive oil. Apply it to dry hair, cover with a shower cap, and wait 15 to 30 minutes. Rinse out, then shampoo and condition as you usually do.

banana peel

USE TO: Grow healthier roses. Plant a peel at the base of a rosebush, an inch down in the soil. The potassium in the peel feeds the plant and helps fend off diseases.

beach towel

USE TO: Make a summery shower curtain. Hang a boldly patterned pair using clip-on drapery rings.

Chapter 1

bedsheet

USE TO: Keep floors from being scratched when moving furniture. Place a sheet under any heavy piece.
+ Create a backyard shade tent. Drape the sheet over a low-lying branch and tack down the corners with golf tees.
+ Shield a car's seats from drive-through detritus and post-hike mud.
+ Even out a mattress dip. Place as many folded sheets as it takes under the sagging section.
+ Stand in as a runner. Fold a sheet in thirds and center it on the table.
+ Protect clothes from the acid in a cedar chest. Line it with a sheet that has been washed without bleach or fabric softener, which can possibly damage fabrics.

berry basket

USE TO: Corral bathroom essentials.

binder clip

USE TO: Give your wallet the day off. Thread keys through the "arms" and use the clip to hold bills and credit cards.
+ Display photos. Stand clips on their flat ends and place pics between the two arms.
+ Keep window-blind cords out of the reach of little hands (or paws). Gather cords at a safe level and clasp.
+ Organize a linen closet. The big clips can keep matching sets of sheets together.

birdbath

USE TO: Swap birdsong for blooms. Plant flowering succulents in an underused birdbath.
+ Hold ice and bottled drinks for a garden party.

bleach

USE TO: Extend the life of cut flowers. Add a dash to the vase water.

bleach bottle

USE TO: Outfit a home gym. Fill two with sand and use as dumbbells.
+ Make a scoop for soil or cat litter. Cut the bottle in half and toss the base.
+ Designate safe swimming areas. Tie a few empty bottles to a rope.
+ Make yourself heard. Cut off the bottom and use the bottle part as a megaphone.

◄ bobby pin

USE TO: Mark your page in a thriller.
+ Keep pleats folded while ironing tricky pieces.

book cover

USE TO: Avoid looking like a tourist. When you're out exploring unfamiliar areas, tuck the telltale guidebook inside a different title's cover to check directions more discreetly.

bowl

USE TO: Peel garlic. Place cloves in a bowl, cover it with another bowl to form a sphere, and shake. The papery skins will flake right off.

bracelet

USE TO: Dress up a napkin when a plain napkin ring simply won't do.

branches

USE TO: Make an instant holiday centerpiece. Place a few branches in a tall vase and decorate with ornaments.
+ Spruce up a wrapped gift. Tuck pretty sprigs into the ribbon in place of a bow.

bread

USE TO: Clean an oil painting. Softly rub a piece of white bread over it to remove dust or dirt.

brooch

USE TO: Decorate the refrigerator. Remove the pin with a wire cutter, glue a magnet to the back of the brooch, and post those grocery lists and photos in style.
+ Turn a cardigan into a formfitting wrap sweater. Pull one side across the body and pin it in place.

broom

USE TO: Dust way-up-there crown moldings and other cobweb-collecting crannies. Place a microfiber rag over the bristles if you like.

Bubble Wrap

USE TO: Keep fruits and vegetables from getting knocked around. Line the produce drawer with a sheet.
+ Pack jewelry for a trip. To help tangle-prone necklaces and bracelets arrive knot-free, tape them on a length of wrap and roll tightly.

bucket

USE TO: Hold cocktails. At outdoor parties, turn over a bucket to create a small impromptu side table.

Bundt pan

USE TO: Make an ice ring for a punch bowl. Freeze water in the pan, then pop out the ring to chill the beverage in place of cubes.
+ Cut corn from the cob without the mess. Place an ear in the center of the pan. As you slide the knife down, the corn will fall right into the pan.

business-card case

USE TO: Transport sweetener packets for a just-how-you-like-it caffeine jolt, no matter where you are.

business-card organizer

USE TO: Showcase favorite wallet-size photographs, or make a time line of school portraits.

+ Keep club and gift cards in order. File them alphabetically so the next time you're ready to treat yourself at Target, you'll know exactly where to turn.

button ▶

USE TO: Replace wayward board-game pieces without missing a beat (or a turn).

button bag

USE TO: Attain your RDAs on the go. Carry your daily dose of vitamins in one of those mini zippered plastic bags that extra buttons come in.

MASTER MULTITASKER / **BAKING SODA** / **1** Sprinkle it on a damp sponge to erase crayon, pencil, and ink from painted surfaces. **2 To freshen a stale carpet, scatter soda on it, wait a few hours, then vacuum.** **3** Remove stains on enameled cast-iron pans with a soft nylon brush and a thick paste of baking soda and water. For stainless steel, use a soft cloth and 4 tablespoons of soda in 1 quart of water. **4 Brush teeth with a paste of soda and water.** **5** Pour ½ cup soda, then ½ cup vinegar, down a clogged drain. Cover it with a wet cloth, wait 5 minutes, uncover, and flush with steaming-hot water. **6 To clean minor oil spills in the garage, sprinkle on soda and scrub with a wet brush.** **7** To restore tarnished silver's shine, wash it, then place it on a piece of foil in a pot. Cover the silver with ¼ cup soda, a few teaspoons of salt, and 1 quart boiling water and leave it for a few seconds. **8 Rub tub stains with a paste of equal parts baking soda and cream of tartar and a little lemon juice. Let sit for 30 minutes, then rinse.**

cake dome to cupcake liner ▶

cake dome

USE TO: Make a terrarium. (Covering small potted plants speeds growth.)

cake stand

USE TO: Create a pretty centerpiece. Perch a cluster of different-size pillar and votive candles on top.
+ Glam up a bathroom or bedroom vanity. Put out soaps and washcloths on a stand, or use it to showcase your prettiest perfume bottles.
+ Display treasures, like seashells from your last vacation.
+ Curb countertop clutter. Drop keys and bills on the stand instead.

can

USE TO: Cut dough. Make uniform biscuits or perfectly round cookies with a clean six-ounce tomato-paste or 10-ounce soup can.

can opener

USE TO: Open clamshell packaging without cursing. Run a rotary opener around the pack, starting at a corner.

candle

USE TO: Release a stuck zipper. Rub a candle end along both sides of the metal teeth.
+ Take the tears out of chopping an onion. The flame burns off some of the fumes and disperses the rest.
+ Loosen a hard-to-open drawer. Slide a candle along the drawer bottom's outer edges.
+ Spillproof a recipe card. Rub a thin coat of wax over it.

candy canes

USE TO: Create sweet cupcake toppers. Form hearts by placing mini canes hook to hook and tail to tail on a nonstick baking sheet. Bake at 350° F for 2 to 4 minutes, or until they stick together when you carefully pinch the ends. Cool, remove with a spatula, and place on top of an iced cupcake.

cappuccino maker

USE TO: Speed up breakfast prep. Crack an egg into a coffee mug, whip it with a fork, then insert the foamer (do not use the milk-uptake valve). The steam cooks the egg in seconds.

car wax

USE TO: Preserve a pristine stovetop. Rub on a thin layer before cooking, then wipe off. Spills will lift off easily.
+ Polish dull sinks and faucets.
+ Unstick garden shears. Rub a little paste on the hinge to prevent jams.

carrots

USE TO: Revitalize and deepen the color of red hair. Cut 2 large carrots into big pieces and boil in 2 cups water. Reduce heat and simmer until the water has turned orange; cool. Remove carrots and pour the water over dry hair. Put on a shower cap and wait 20 minutes. Rinse, then use a mild shampoo and conditioner.

cassette case ▶

USE TO: Extend the life of earbuds. Roll up the cord to prevent tangles.

cast-iron pan

USE TO: Display recipes, shopping lists, and anything else your brain is too, well, fried to remember. Hang one on a kitchen wall and swipe magnets from the refrigerator.

CD

USE TO: Stop wet glasses from laying down tracks on the tabletop. (Some CDs are more enjoyable as coasters.)
+ Catch messy candle drips. Rest a pillar candle on top of a CD placed shiny side–up to reflect the glow.
+ Make jazzy (or rockin') invitations. Jot down party details on the shiny side and mail the CD out in a cushioned envelope (postage: about a dollar).

◄ chalk

USE TO: Slow the tarnish on the good silver. Tie up a few pieces of chalk in cheesecloth and store them with the cutlery to absorb moisture.
+ Protect clothes in the closet from mildew. Hang a mesh bag holding a package of chalk near them.
+ Save your picnic-table spread—or windowsill—from marauding ants. Drawing a thick chalk line around either one will repel the critters.

Champagne flutes

USE TO: Elevate simple votives. Place candles atop a cluster of upside-down thick-walled flutes for instant (if tipsy!) ambience.

changing table

USE TO: Create a potting station. Give it a coat of semi- or high-gloss paint to protect it from the elements. Stack pots on shelves, and stash seeds in drawers. Fill an easy-access hanging nylon or canvas diaper bag with shears and gloves.

checkbook

USE TO: Size up a piece of flea-market furniture. Checkbooks are roughly six inches long, making them ideal on-the-go measuring devices.

child's skirt

USE TO: Make a smock for a budding artist. Fashion shoulder straps from rickrack or ribbon, and stitch the ends to the front and back of the skirt's waist.

chip clip

USE TO: Keep jackets from slipping off their hangers. With one of these rubberized grips at each shoulder, the threads stay wrinkle-free and the closet floor stays tidy.

chopstick

USE TO: Level flour in a measuring cup. Leave a chopstick in the flour canister and you won't have to rummage for—or wash—a knife.
+ Ensure that you roll a uniform pie-crust. The dough should be as thick as the widest part of a chopstick.
+ Remove the lint buildup from a clothes dryer's vent.

citrus peel

USE TO: Deodorize a garbage disposal. Drop a few fragrant peels down the drain and flip the switch.

+ Serve sorbet in a memorable way. Slice a citrus fruit in half, scoop out the insides, and freeze the shells to use as bowls. Cut a thin slice from the bottom (without creating a hole) to give each shell a level base.

+ Remove coffee or tea stains from a mug. Rub them with a lightly salted peel from an orange or a lemon.

+ Kick-start a fire. Collect dried peels for kindling.

+ Avoid rock-hard brown sugar. Preserve the moisture by dropping a few inches of orange peel into the bag.

+ Keep pesky cats out of your garden bed. Throw a few peels by your buds. (Cats hate the smell of citrus.)

clothespin ▶

USE TO: Avoid hammer accidents when hanging a picture. Hold a nail securely in place with a clothespin instead of with your finger and thumb.

+ Track guests' towels. When "his" and "hers" don't cover it, give visitors color-coded pins (or write their names on wooden ones) to attach to their bath towels.

+ Support vines in the garden. Make sure they can pass through the holes in the pins as they climb their poles.

+ Turn your refrigerator into a memo board. Glue a magnet to the back of a pin and use it to hold notes, photos, and invitations.

+ Prop up place cards. Paint the pins to go with the place settings.

+ Hold the page in a cookbook while you're busy mixing ingredients.

+ Keep a retractable cord from rewinding too soon. Just clip the cord near the opening.

club soda

USE TO: Shine cookware and fixtures made of stainless steel. Buff scuffs with a cloth dampened with soda, then wipe dry.

coaster

USE TO: Label a gift. Punch a hole in a cardboard coaster, write the recipient's and your name on it, and tie with twine.

+ Catch drips from the honey jar before they can sticky-up shelves.

coatrack

USE TO: Hold necklaces and bracelets. A wall-mounted rack both stores them and shows them off.

coffee can

USE TO: Organize odds and ends. Clean cans, then nail them to the wall for stashing mail and keys.

+ Protect seedlings. Slip cans (with the lids removed) over the plants.

coffee-can lid

USE TO: Paint like a pro. To make a splatter shield for when you're painting a high surface, cut a slit in the center of a lid and pull the paintbrush through.

+ Dispense twine. Poke a hole in the lid and run the twine through.

+ Monogram walls. Using a utility knife, cut a letter or a shape from the center of a lid to make a handy, durable stencil.

coffee filter

For this Master Multitasker's many uses, see page 36

coffee grinder

USE TO: Convert hunks of dry bread into crumbs.

coffee grounds

USE TO: Exfoliate skin in the shower. Mix 2 tablespoons wet grounds, 1 tablespoon fine salt, and 2 tablespoons olive oil and massage into the skin in a circular motion.

coffee mug

USE TO: Perk up your mornings in a caffeine-free way. Grow a houseplant in a large mug. (Add a bit of gravel to the bottom for drainage.)

coffeemaker

USE TO: Soften chocolate for baking. Put it in an oven-proof bowl set on the heating plate and turn on the machine.

◄ colander

USE TO: Sift flour.

+ Hand launder delicates. A colander shields them from any residue in the sink that can harm the fabric, such as peroxide from toothpaste or caustic agents from cleansers.

+ Fend off annoying flies at a picnic. Upend a wire-mesh colander over a tray of food.

+ Make ice cubes last longer at your next cocktail party. Put them in a colander set into a bowl. As they melt, the water will drain through the holes instead of sitting and turning the ice to slush.

+ Create soft, dappled lighting. Set tealights inside a metal colander and place it above eye level.

comb

USE TO: Decorate a cake. Lightly glide a (clean!) comb over just-applied frosting to create ridges.

+ Etch a striated pattern in still-wet wall paint.

+ Fluff up a spot in the carpet that has been squashed by a furniture leg.

+ Make a kazoo. Fold parchment paper over the teeth, press your lips lightly to the paper, and hum.

+ Strain broken bits of cork from wine. Hold a fine-tooth comb over the bottle's mouth as you pour.

+ Depill a sweater.

contact-lens case

USE TO: Carry pills in your purse for an overnight stay.
+ Pack small amounts of salt, pepper, and spices for a camping trip.

conversation hearts

USE TO: Mark out a hopscotch course in the driveway or jot down messages on a memo board, since the candies double as chalk.

cookie cutter

USE TO: Personalize a pillar candle with an initial, a word, or a shape. Hold the candle steady, position the cutter, and tap it lightly with a hammer.
+ Add flourishes to a cake. Place open (handleless) cookie cutters on top and fill with sprinkles, powdered sugar, or cocoa powder.
+ Hang with ribbon as a tree ornament.

cooking spray

USE TO: Set a manicure fast. Lightly mist newly painted nails for instant smudge protection.
+ Make cleaning candleholders a breeze. Spritz the inside before inserting a votive. After the candle burns down, the wax will easily lift out.
+ Prevent buildup on a shovel. Spray both sides before getting to work.
+ Coat a grater so cheese glides off.

cork ▶

USE TO: Make a compact sewing kit. Just stick in needles and pins, then wrap it with a few lengths of thread.
+ Pamper your floors. Slice a cork into disks and glue one to each foot of heavy or often-moved furniture.
+ Marry pairs of earrings. Stick the posts into a cork to keep them together.
+ Protect hands from a hot pot-lid handle. Slip a cork under it, grip that with your fingers, and lift.
+ Cap an X-Acto knife before tossing it into a drawer.
+ Get a blaze crackling faster. Keep corks in rubbing alcohol in a sealed jar (stored away from the fireplace, of course). Just before lighting a fire, toss a few in under the kindling.
+ Silence slamming cabinet doors. Glue thin slices of cork to the inside corners.

corkboard

USE TO: Hang jewelry or hair accessories from thumbtacks.

cornstarch

USE TO: Lift grease from fabrics or carpets. Cover the spill with cornstarch, wait 15 to 30 minutes, then vacuum.
+ Balance the oiliness of moisturizing makeup. Brush on a thin layer as a finishing touch.

cotton balls

USE TO: Help hollow-stemmed cut flowers, like gerberas, stay hydrated. Cut a stem at a 45-degree angle, fill it with water, then plug the end with a piece of cotton.
+ Protect the tips of dishwashing gloves. Place a ball in each fingertip so long nails won't poke through.

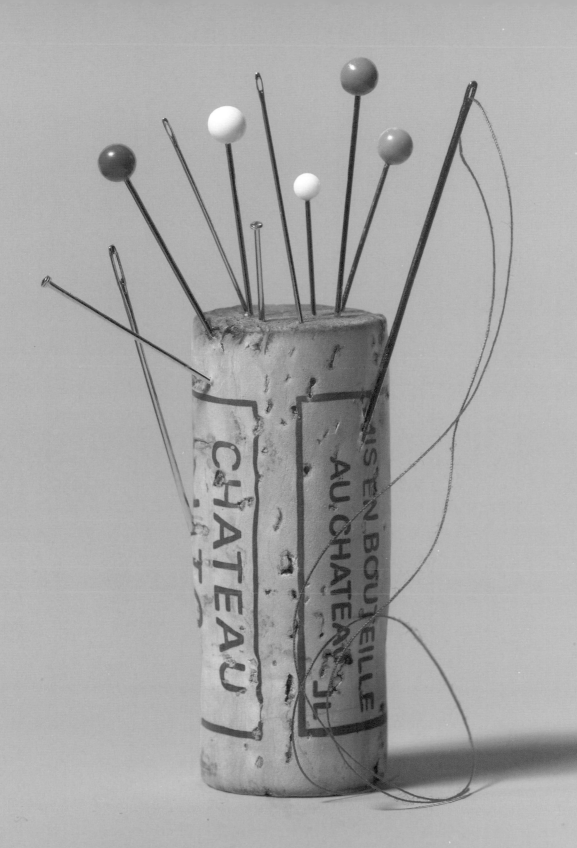

coupon

USE TO: Ward off temper tantrums in the supermarket. Hand out coupons you don't need and start a game of I Spy. First one to spot five items gets a big prize (OK, a pack of bubble gum) at the checkout counter.

coverlet

USE TO: Revamp a sofa that has seen better days. Center the coverlet, leaving at least three inches of it puddling on the floor in front of the sofa. Use a wooden spoon to tuck the fabric deep between the cushions, smoothing as you go. Fold back excess material at the front edges of the sofa and pin it underneath.

crayons

USE TO: Create an inspiring tool for craft projects. Drop several peeled crayons of various shades into each cup of a greased muffin tin. Place it in the oven for 4 minutes at 400° F. Result: big, round, multi-colored crayons.

credit card

USE TO: Smooth out pesky air bubbles from contact paper or stickers.

+ Unstick hard-to-get-at, stuck-on grease around oven knobs.
+ Remove wax from wood without scratching. Harden the wax with an ice cube wrapped in a plastic bag, then use the card to scrape it off.

croquet wickets

USE TO: Stake a garden hose. Place the wickets in the ground, then run a hose through them.

◄ **cupcake carrier**

USE TO: Keep office supplies, jewelry, and other small things in order. The carrier's snap-on top keeps them all under cover.

cupcake liner

USE TO: Serve ice cream at parties without the drips. Freeze individual scoops in liners the night before.

+ Transform a string of lights into a pretty garland. Poke each bulb through a foil liner.
+ Show what a creative Halloween party "ghost-ess" you are. Turn white liners upside down, attach googly eyes, and display them by the boo-fet.
+ Create a winter wonderland in the entryway. Flatten white paper liners (foil ones will work, too), fold into halves or quarters, then snip out small shapes along the folds. When you open them back up, voilà! Snowflakes you can string from the ceiling.

MASTER MULTITASKER / COFFEE FILTER / 1 When snapping a close-up, soften the brightness for a more flattering photo by placing a paper coffee filter over the flash. **2 Protect hands from a drippy Popsicle by pushing the sticks through the middle of a filter.** **3** Use a filter to buff streaks from a mirror or a window. **4 Serve chips, popcorn, or cookies in filters for portable portions.** **5** To strain yogurt, fasten a filter to the top of a deep cup or jar with a rubber band, then slowly pour in plain yogurt. Let it drain for an hour. **6 Shield stacked china from scratches and nicks by layering a filter between each piece.** **7** When its cork crumbles, salvage a bottle of wine by slowly pouring it through a filter into a pitcher or a carafe. **8 A circular filter is perfect for carrying tacos or sandwiches around at a party.** **9** Prevent messes on microwave walls by covering splatter-prone foods with a filter. **10 Place one over a flowerpot's drainage hole to prevent soil from leaking out.**

denture tablet to dustpan ▶

denture tablet

USE TO: Do away with red-wine dregs in a decanter. Fill one with warm water, drop in a tablet, and let it dissolve.

deodorant

USE TO: Make breaking in shoes less of a pain. Rub clear stick deodorant on spots prone to blistering before you step out in a stiff new pair.

desk-file organizer ▶

USE TO: Sort cookie sheets, cutting boards, and jelly-roll pans by size or material for easy access in a cabinet.
+ Line up LPs for a vinyl version of a party playlist.

dictionary

USE TO: Make gift wrap that speaks volumes. Blow up an entry that relates to the occasion (for Valentine's Day, try *kiss* or *love*) and use a highlighter to mark your most heartfelt sentiments.

digital camera

USE TO: Rig up an emergency flashlight. Take a photo of a bare white wall; if the power goes out, call up the picture to illuminate your path.
+ Navigate a foreign city. Take pictures of subway maps, street signs, and neighborhood details. When you need to find your way (or remember where you spotted that cute shop), just scroll to the appropriate shot.

dish rack

USE TO: Organize drawing pads and coloring books, and corral crayons, pencils, pens, and markers in the silverware basket.

dish towel

USE TO: Make a cutting board stay put. Placing a damp towel under the board will keep it from shifting.
+ Improve on the standard hostess gift. Wrap a bottle of wine with a patterned dish towel, held in place with a ribbon or a pin.
+ Set a bistro-style table. Enlist colorful dish towels as washing machine–friendly place mats.

+ Steam rice. Once boiled rice is tender, remove the pan from the heat, put a folded cotton towel over it, replace the lid, and set aside for 5 to 10 minutes. The towel will absorb the excess moisture—great rice, no mush.
+ Fashion an apron. Sew a button to each corner of one long side of a dish towel. Tie a long piece of ribbon around each button and knot. Wrap the ribbons around your waist and tie a bow.
+ Whip up a dog toy. Find three old towels. Cut an inch-wide strip from one short end of two of them. Use one strip to tie the three towels firmly together at one end. Tightly braid them, then tie the other end with the second strip.

dishwasher

USE TO: Clean loads of surprising items:
+ action figures (top rack, in a mesh laundry bag)
+ baseball caps (they can bend out of shape in the washing machine)
+ ceramic cabinet knobs (in basket)
+ fan grilles, switch plates, and vent covers (plastic, aluminum, or steel)
+ flip-flops (top rack)
+ hairbrushes and combs (not those made from wood or boar bristle)
+ knee pads, shin guards, and mouth guards (top rack)
+ light-fixture covers (top rack, but not if they're painted, enameled, or antiqued)
+ potatoes (top rack, rinse-only cycle)—quicker than scrubbing when you're doing mashed for 20.

+ rain boots (positioned horizontally, liners removed)
+ tools with metal or plastic handles

double-sided tape

USE TO: Keep the tail end of a belt from flopping around. Secure it with a small piece of tape.
+ Fix a fallen hem when there's no time for a trip to the tailor.
+ Anchor an outdoor tablecloth to a picnic table.

dryer lint

USE TO: Entertain the kids on laundry day. To make a "dough" they can sculpt into blocks, animals, or anything else, combine 3 cups dryer lint (pulled apart), 2 cups water, 1 cup flour, and ½ teaspoon vegetable oil in a pot. Stir continuously over low heat until the mixture is smooth and binds together. Pour it onto wax paper to cool.

dryer sheet

For this Master Multitasker's many uses, see page 44.

duct tape

USE TO: Safely loosen a hard-to-remove lightbulb (like a recessed bulb). Press the center of a foot-long strip of tape to the middle of the bulb. Fold each loose end in half so it sticks to itself. Gripping each end between a thumb and an index finger, give a counterclockwise twist to loosen the bulb.

+ Lay out a rainproof hopscotch outline on the driveway.
+ Reinforce a piece of sandpaper. Stick tape to the back so the paper won't tear as easily.
+ Make a suitcase a lot easier to identify. Stick a few pieces of duct tape to the sides to avoid the tedious "Is *that* mine?" routine at the baggage carousel.
+ Patch torn umbrellas and tents.

◄ dustpan

USE TO: Clean up after playtime. Scoop up small figurines and toys (and dump them directly into a storage chest).

MASTER MULTITASKER / DRYER SHEET / 1 To loosen caked-on food, place one in a pan, then fill with warm water and soak overnight. **2 Banish musty smells from books by slipping a dryer sheet between a few pages. 3** To pick up pet hair from furniture, swipe a sheet over Spot's favorite spot. **4 A sheet at the bottom of a gym bag helps tamp down odors. 5** In place of a sachet in a drawer, try a scented dryer sheet. **6 Help shoes smell fresher by storing a sheet inside each one. (You may want to double up for Dad's sneakers.) 7** To stop static cling on clothes—or tame flyaway hair—rub a sheet over the problem area. **8 Sawdust on a basement workstation comes up fast with one pass of a wipe. 9** Press an iron (on a low setting) over a dryer sheet until any residue on the plate disappears. **10 To prevent tangles, run a threaded needle through a sheet before you begin stitching. 11** Use a dryer sheet to dust venetian blinds without kicking up a cloud.

earring to eyeglass case ▶

earring

USE TO: Repair eyeglasses in a pinch (without resorting to tape). If a screw is lost, use a stud to connect the arm to the frame, then secure it with the earring's back.

+ Give plain flat shoes a sparkly kick. Top them with a pair of matching clip-on earrings.

+ Dress up an inspiration board. Put stray posts to work as one-of-a-kind pushpins.

Easter egg (plastic)

USE TO: Store portion-controlled snack servings.

egg carton

USE TO: Create a custom palette for an afternoon art session.

egg slicer

USE TO: Cut strawberries, mozzarella, and mushrooms into neat slivers.

eggshells

USE TO: Get to the bottom of dirty bottles and vases. Swirl crushed shells, warm water, and a drop of dishwashing liquid around in a narrow vase, then rinse.

electrical tape

USE TO: Liven up a child's chair with colorful stripes.

+ Wrap a tennis racket's grip for extra cushioning.

+ Create an easy "frame" for a kid's artwork. Just tape all around the edges. Unlike real frames, one roll of tape fits all.

+ Make geometric patterns on a clear shower curtain.

emery board

USE TO: Gently buff stains from suede.

Epsom salts

USE TO: Fertilize your houseplants. Encourage green growth by watering with a solution of 2 tablespoons salt to 1 gallon of water once a month.

+ Remove greasy buildup from hair. Add 1 tablespoon salt to 1 cup of water and massage into hair. Rinse well.

essential oil

USE TO: Clean combs and brushes. Fill a bowl with 1½ cups water, ½ cup distilled white vinegar, and 20 drops of tea-tree, lavender, or eucalyptus oil. Soak combs and brushes for 20 minutes, rinse, then air-dry.

+ Cut down on soap-scum buildup on glass shower doors. Wipe with a few drops of lemon oil twice a month.

+ Restore scuffed floors. Apply a few drops of tea-tree oil to damaged areas, wipe up excess oil, and rub in distilled white vinegar.

+ Get rid of toilet stains. Fill a spray bottle with 2 teaspoons tea-tree oil and 2 cups water and shake. Spritz along the bowl's inside rim. Let sit for 30 minutes, then scrub.

+ Wash windows. Remove grime with a mixture of 2 ounces of water and 10 drops of lavender or lemongrass oil. (The oils may even repel houseflies!)

eyeglass case ▶

USE TO: Keep nail files, clippers, and other manicure supplies at hand.

+ Pack makeup brushes for a trip.

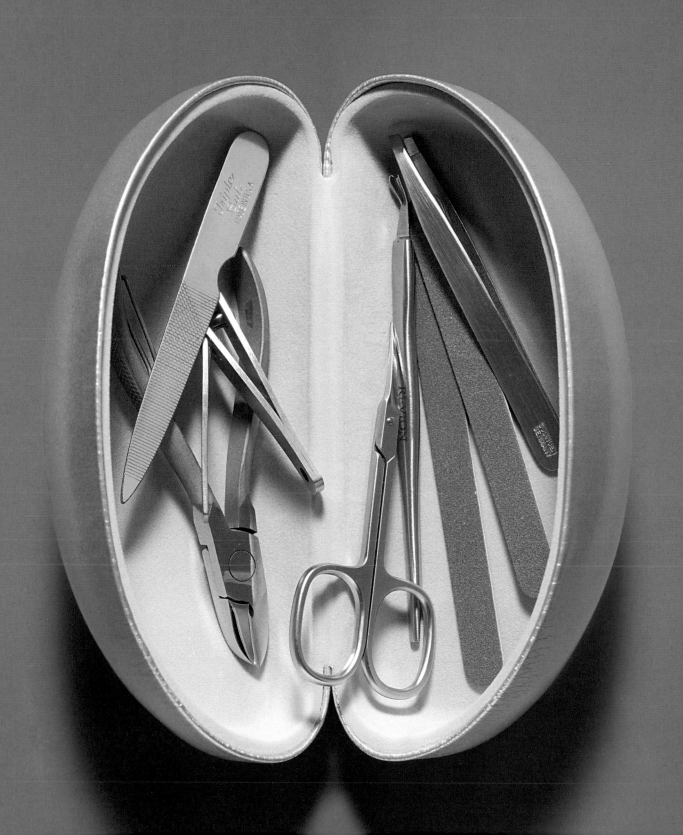

felt circles to funnel ▶

felt circles

USE TO: Protect wall paint. Stick circles to the corners at the back of a heavy mirror or frame.
+ Anchor a cutting board's corners.
+ Silence banging cabinet doors. Place a circle on the inside corner of each door so you can sneak midnight snacks undetected.
+ Help your strappy garments stay put. Affix a circle to each end of a hanger.

film canister

USE TO: Dispense stamps. Cut a slit in the side and thread the end of the roll through it.

+ Assemble a mobile manicure fix. Cut a sponge up into small pieces, saturate them with nail-polish remover, then place them in the canister.

flat iron

USE TO: Get the kinks out of ribbons and other trims. Use a low heat setting.
+ Avoid hauling out the ironing board. Set this hair-straightening tool to low heat and tackle minor touch-ups, like smoothing out the areas between a shirt's buttons.

floatie

USE TO: Get that souvenir Burgundy home safely. Slip a child's water wing over a bottle and partially inflate it to cushion your precious cargo.

floss

For this Master Multitasker's many uses, see page 54.

flour

USE TO: Polish brass or copper. Make a paste of equal parts flour and salt with a few tablespoons of white vinegar.

flower frog

USE TO: Make a desktop display that's as fresh as a daisy. Instead of blooms, slip snapshots or mementos between the device's teeth.

fork

USE TO: Regulate the flow from an oil bottle. Instead of removing the foil seal, just poke holes in it.

+ Puree garlic. Hold the tines flat against a work surface and vigorously rub a peeled clove across them.
+ Fluff up flattened carpet pile.

frame

USE TO: Construct a picture-perfect memo board. Replace the glass and photograph with a sheet of cork.
+ Make a chic serving tray. Attach handles to the two shorter edges of a wood frame and slide a pretty piece of gift wrap under the glass.

funnel ▶

USE TO: Dispense yarn or twine. Place the spool inside the funnel and pull the end through the hole for smooth (tangle-free) crafting.

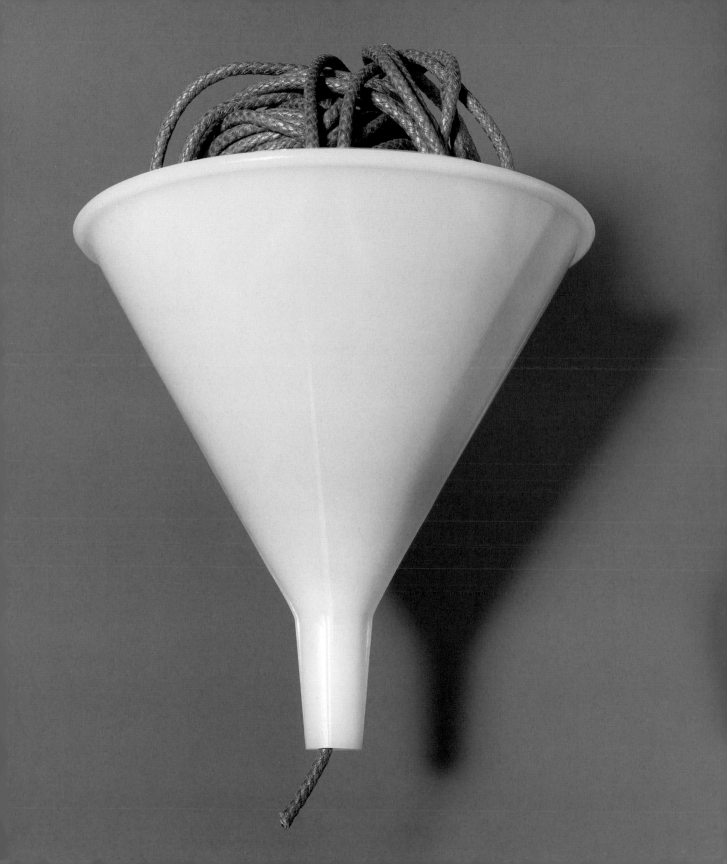

MASTER MULTITASKER / FLOSS (UNWAXED) / 1 Until you can get to the jeweler, rethread the beads of a broken necklace with floss, tie the ends to the original findings, and knot the ends several times. **2 Safely loosen a photograph stuck to an album page or another photo by sliding a piece of floss between the two. 3** Use dental floss to slice cheesecake, soft cheese, or hard-boiled eggs with the greatest of ease. Wrap a piece tightly around one finger of each hand, hold firmly, and press down. **4 String a sturdier popcorn garland when the holidays roll around. 5** Use floss to hang a lightweight frame (without glass). At the top of the back, attach a screw to each side. Wrap one end of a strand of floss several times around one screw and knot. Then, leaving some slack, wrap and knot the other end to the second screw. Hang the picture from a nail. **6 Truss a turkey or a chicken with floss (if you forgot to pick up twine).**

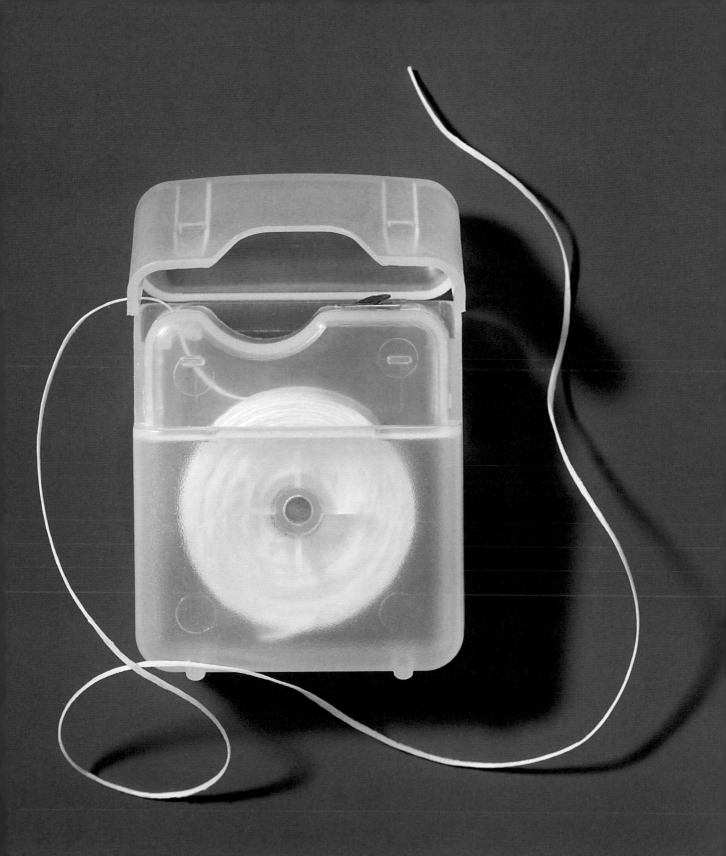

garden-hose rack

USE TO: Streamline your holiday decorating. Wrap strings of lights around the rack so they stay tangle-free (and you stay stress-free).

garden spade

USE TO: Break up large chunks from a bag of ice. The (clean) handheld spade then doubles as a scoop.

gardening gloves

USE TO: Clean blinds and shutters. When they don't need the full treatment, wipe off dust and dirt with a pair of cotton gloves.

garlic press

USE TO: Crack cumin and coriander seeds and peppercorns.

+ Make Play-Doh "hair" for kids' clay creatures. Just fill the chamber and squeeze.

gift box

USE TO: Transport cupcakes. Slice X's into the lid and pop the sweet treats in them for safe traveling.

ginger

USE TO: Soothe blisters and burns. Grate fresh ginger and squeeze the juice directly onto the sore spots.

glow-in-the-dark stars

USE TO: Light the way to the bathroom. Help a little one navigate at night by creating a comforting hallway constellation.

golf tees

USE TO: Decode a potluck dinner. Distinguish vegetarian dishes from meat ones— or medium-rare from medium— by flagging them with colored tees.

grapefruit knife

USE TO: Make gardening work easy to dig. The curved blade is handy for pulling weeds in container gardens or tight spaces, where traditional tools are too big for the job.

grater ▶

USE TO: Strain citrus. Squeeze a fruit over a flat grater to keep seeds out of the juice.
+ Salvage burned muffins or cookies (and your reputation in the kitchen). Lightly grate away the charred bits and no one will be the wiser.

greeting card

USE TO: Label presents. Cut out pretty portions of cards you've received and recycle them as gift tags. If you like, make a tie by punching a hole in a corner, running a string or embroidery thread through, and knotting it.

hair clip to hydrogen peroxide ▶

hair clip

USE TO: Maintain some modesty at the gym. The claws will help hold a post-shower towel in place.

hair conditioner

USE TO: Shave legs—and make your carry-on load one product lighter.

hair dryer

USE TO: Remove price stickers without chipping your nails. A shot of hot air quickly loosens a label.
+ Give store-bought plastic eyeglass frames a custom fit. Heat them with a dryer, then mold the plastic to suit your face.
+ Safely remove candle drips from wood furniture. Blow on medium until wax starts to melt, then wipe away with a cloth.

+ Add gloss to cake frosting. Hit it with a quick blast.

hair elastic ▶

USE TO: Bolster a bouquet. After you've positioned the buds as you want them, wrap a clear band around the stems to keep them that way.

hair spray

USE TO: Simplify threading a needle. Spray the thread end to stiffen it and prevent fraying.
+ Stop static cling. Aim a quick spritz at the sticking point.

handkerchief

USE TO: Wrap a gift. A pretty embroidered hankie helps a small box make a bigger statement.

high chair

USE TO: Expand your counter space. Enlist a clip-on version for rounding up keys and mail.

hosiery

USE TO: Erase deodorant marks on clothing with a quick rub.
+ Revive a dusty candle. Pop it into a stocking, roll it around a bit, and it's ready to glow.
+ Keep a hairbrush clean. Stretch a piece of hose over the bristles, push it to the base, and trim to fit. Remove it when the brush is dirty and all the lint and buildup will go with it.

hot water

USE TO: Keep syrup from sticking to measuring spoons and cups. Run them under hot water so viscous substances, such as molasses, honey, and syrup, will slide off easily.
+ Loosen a stuck metal jar lid. The heat causes the metal to expand, making twist-off a snap.

hydrogen peroxide

USE TO: Disinfect a keyboard. A cotton swab dipped in peroxide gets into all the nooks and crannies.

ice cream cone to ironing-board cupboard ▶

ice cream cone

USE TO: Serve cupcakes in an unexpected way. Fill 24 flat-bottom cones two-thirds full with cake batter. Place them in two high-sided 9-by-13-inch baking pans and bake one pan at a time on the center rack at 325° F for 30 minutes. Let cool, then frost. Sprinkles optional.

ice cream scoop ▶

USE TO: Dole out dry ingredients. Most standard scoops double as ¼-cup measuring devices. **+** Train the next generation of cookie maestros to make perfect dollops of dough every time.

ice cube

USE TO: Revive stale bread. Rub an ice cube across an unsliced loaf until the crust is damp, then bake at 375° F for 12 minutes.

ice-cube tray

For this Master Multitasker's many uses, see page 68.

ice gel pack

USE TO: Help Pinot Grigio keep its cool at a picnic. Wrap the pack around a bottle of white wine and secure it with a string or a rubber band.

ice scraper

USE TO: Lift sticky pastry dough from a work surface.

+ Hide all your picture-hanging mistakes. The handy winter car tool pinch-hits to smooth wall filler into nail holes and small cracks.

icing

USE TO: Stabilize a layer cake. Dab a bit of icing on the serving plate before adding the layers.

ink pad

USE TO: Avoid licking stamps (and destroying your taste buds) when holiday-card season arrives. Replace a dried-out ink pad with a damp sponge and use it to seal envelopes and affix stamps.

iron

USE TO: Whip up a grilled cheese in a dorm room. With an iron set on medium, lightly press a sandwich between parchment paper sheets for a few minutes per side until the cheese is melted.

ironing board

USE TO: Expand the serving area for extended-family feasts. Cover the board with a tablecloth to create an extra buffet for light items (no ice buckets or weighty beverages, please).

ironing-board cupboard

USE TO: Organize spices. Repurpose a cupboard that's no longer needed by installing narrow wood shelves with L-brackets, then adding front rails so spices stay put.

MASTER MULTITASKER / **ICE-CUBE TRAY** / **1** Freeze aloe-vera gel into single-serving sunburn relief. The cubes cool the heat instantly, then the soothing aloe gets to work. **2 Use a tray for quick access to earrings, rings, and necklaces. 3** The cubbies are great for organizing desk supplies, like thumbtacks and paper clips, or sewing notions, like buttons. **4 To make a batch of identical-sized cookies, roll the dough out flat, then press an upside-down tray into it. 5** For a suppertime shortcut, freeze extra broth, pesto, or other sauces in trays, then transfer the cubes to a freezer-safe bag. **6 Fill trays with sprinkles, nuts, and other toppings for a self-serve sundae bar. 7** Instead of watering down drinks with melting ice, cool them more tastefully with citrus cubes. Squeeze lemons and limes, pour the juices into trays, and freeze. **8 The compartments of a plastic tray make perfect pots for mixing watercolors at craft time.**

jar to jump rope ▶

jar

USE TO: Store tissues. Ditch the generic paper box and dispense tissues from a jar instead.
+ Clear a work surface. Place bits and pieces—thumbtacks, nails, whatever seems to be all over the place—in a jar. Use Super Glue to fix the lid to the underside of a desk, table, or cabinet, then screw the jar into the lid to whisk clutter up, up, and away.
+ Provide garden-party ambience. Pop votive candles into Mason jars and line them up along pathways like luminarias. Or wrap the rims securely with wire, making a hook on the end so you can hang the candles from branches for a little midsummer-night magic.

jelly-roll pan

USE TO: Make Thanksgiving prep a little less messy. Place the turkey on a jelly-roll pan when you're ready to carve. The juices will collect there instead of on the countertop.

jewel case

USE TO: Keep your mother's marinara off the recipe you have yet to memorize. Set a jewel case on the counter with the lid standing up, then slip the index card inside to protect it from spatters.

+ Identify dishes at a potluck or a buffet. Slip a label (with potential-allergen alerts) inside a case next to each dish.
+ Scrape ice from the car windshield when a sudden snowstorm catches you unprepared.
+ Keep beads from rolling every which way at craft time. For tiny beads, place a strip of double-sided tape inside the jewel-case cover and stick them there until you're ready for them.
+ Assign seating at a holiday dinner. Slide a festive photograph of each family member into a case and prop it in front of his or her place setting.

jewelry box

USE TO: Store easily misplaced game pieces. Place dice and tokens in the small compartments, play money in the large one, and coins and chips in the ring slots.

jump rope ▶

USE TO: Give a child's present a boost. Tie a rope around it instead of pretty (but predictable) ribbon for a fun twist—and an extra gift.

kazoo to knob ▶

kazoo

USE TO: Make a two-in-one toy. Dip the end into soapy water and blow for a sudsy symphony of bubbles.

ketchup

USE TO: Restore the shine and refresh the color of copper cookware. Smear a thin layer onto tarnished pots with a cloth or a paper towel. After five minutes, rinse with warm water and towel-dry.

ketchup bottle

USE TO: Driplessly parcel out pancake batter. Pour it into a clean bottle, then squeeze onto the pan, whether in plate-size rounds or silver dollars (with or without Mickey Mouse ears).
+ Decorate dinner plates. Squirt on squiggles, dots, and rings of sauce like the pros.
+ Store homemade salad dressing or flavored syrups for fancy coffee drinks.

key protector

USE TO: Quiet Fido's comings and goings. Cover jingling dog tags with rubber key protectors.

kiddie pool

USE TO: Keep drinks on ice at a party.
+ Bring the beach right to your backyard. Fill a pool with sand, keep the garden hose nearby, and host a castle-building competition.

kite

USE TO: Soften a too-bright lighting fixture in a kid's room. Suspend a kite from the ceiling or the fixture so that the fabric drapes a few inches below the light's cover.

knife

USE TO: Weigh down a window treatment. Open one end of the bottom hem and slide in a butter knife to keep the fabric from taking flight.

knitting needle ▶

USE TO: Neatly open an envelope. Slide the tip under the flap.
+ Assist young vines with their vertical progress. Plant a needle in the soil and tie a stem to it.

knob

USE TO: Make magazine files easier to get down from high shelves. Poke a small hole in a sturdy file with the tip of a pair of sharp scissors, push in a drawer pull, and secure it with a screw and a nut.

laundry basket to lunch box ▶

laundry basket

USE TO: Tote toys to and from the beach. Sand will sift through the container's holes, so you won't bring it back home.
+ Store a coiled garden hose with the nozzle nestled in the center.
+ Shelter plants during a rain- or hailstorm.

lazy Susan

USE TO: Streamline the Easter egg–decorating process. Instead of passing containers of dye (and risking spills), place them on the turntable.

lemon

For this Master Multitasker's many uses, see page 82.

letter opener

USE TO: Neatly open a cereal-box lid.

lettuce leaf

USE TO: Contain taco fillings. Line the shell with a leaf before ladling in meat and toppings.

Life Savers

USE TO: Ring a birthday cake's candles. They'll catch wax drips while the honoree works up her wish. Use candies from the original-size rolls for a snug fit.

lightbulb

USE TO: Smooth wrinkled ribbon. Run the fabric over a clean, lit bulb. (Use one that has been on for less than five minutes.)

lightbulb carton

USE TO: Protect snapshots. Place prints in a flattened cardboard sleeve to keep them wrinkle- and scratch-free.

lingerie bag

USE TO: Reunite separated socks. Hang the bag in a closet and stash singles there to await their mates.
+ Corral loose plastic lids in the dishwasher.

lint roller ▶

USE TO: Clean up glitter and other tiny craft-time remnants.
+ Dust a fabric lamp shade.

lip balm

USE TO: Keep your shoelaces tied so they won't trip you up. Before tying, dab balm onto the spot where the knot goes and the bow will magically stay put.

+ Treat a cut. A dab of petrolatum-based balm may help it heal faster.
+ Moisturize dry cuticles on the go.

lollipop

USE TO: Stir a cocktail. Try lime pops with vodka tonics or cherry with punch.

luggage tag

USE TO: Avoid decorating mistakes. Tuck fabric, paint, and wallpaper swatches inside, strap the tag to your purse, and hit the shops.
+ Hold a loved one's photo when you're traveling.
+ Stand in for a gift tag.

lunch box

USE TO: Keep toiletries from mucking up everything else in the suitcase. The soft-sided insulated kind is waterproof, and the handle can hang on a hook in the bathroom.

MASTER MULTITASKER / LEMON / 1 To lift stains from a cutting board, rub them with juice, let sit for 20 minutes, then rinse. **2 Keep apple and pear slices from browning by squeezing a little juice over them.** 3 Brighten whites by adding a half cup of juice to the wash cycle. **4 Remove red-wine stains from your lips by rubbing them with lemon juice. Then rinse, dry, and apply lip balm.** 5 Clean tile grout with lemon juice and a teaspoon or two of cream of tartar, then rinse. **6 Feed flowers (and kill bacteria) with the juice of half a lemon, 1 teaspoon sugar, and a few drops of bleach in 1 quart of warm water.** 7 Put out a lemon at a party to collect used toothpicks. (Stick one in ahead of time as a hint.) **8 Whiten fingernails by rubbing them with a lemon wedge.** 9 To clear sticky cheeses from a grater, wipe both sides with a wedge of lemon. **10 Bleach dishwasher-safe containers with a little juice, let dry in a sunny location, then wash.**

magnet to mustard powder

magnet

USE TO: Stop tweezers from going astray. Install a strong magnet on the inside of the medicine-cabinet door and the tool will always be at your fingertips.
+ Keep the garbage in the bag, not at the bottom of the bin. Pin the top edge of a trash bag in place with magnets to foil rubbish's escape plans.
+ Make playful place cards for a dinner party. Raid your child's toy stash for alphabet magnets and mark each guest's spot with his first initial.

magnetic clip

USE TO: Raise a recipe to eye level. Place a card in the clip and stick it to the refrigerator, the stove hood, or a pot rack for easy reading while you work.

magnetic knife strip

USE TO: End the morning scramble to locate your car keys. Hang a strip by the front door and slap the key ring against it the minute you get home.
+ Keep track of your to-do list. Hang the sleek strip in any handy spot (your desk, kitchen, or mud room) along with a batch of magnets.

mailbox

USE TO: Attract flighty neighbors. Nail an old mailbox to a branch and watch house wrens and finches flock to feather their nests in it.

mailing label

USE TO: Lift lint—or pet hair or stray threads—off your outfit. Press the sticky side over your duds before a meeting to polish your presentation.

makeup case

USE TO: Tote kids' art supplies. Now that your travel toiletries have downsized to fit snugly inside a plastic bag, stash crayons and pencils where the makeup brushes used to go, and tuck stickers and stamps into the smaller compartments.

marbles ▶

USE TO: Monitor the double boiler. A few marbles added to the bottom pan will rattle when the water gets low.
+ Add pops of color to a potted plant's topsoil.

marshmallow

USE TO: Prevent brown sugar from hardening. One or two inside the bag should keep it moist.

martini shaker

USE TO: Dispense copious amounts of glitter during craft time.
+ Upgrade iced coffee. Fill the shaker with ice, milk, sugar, and your favorite flavoring. Shake vigorously for a frothy and evenly blended caffeine fix.

masking tape

USE TO: Keep baseboards scuff-free when you vacuum. Cover the edges of the vacuum's head with tape and it won't leave dark smudges when you inevitably bump into the walls.

+ Make a scraper for cocoa (or other dry ingredients) so you get nice, level scoops. Cut one long piece of tape and one the width of the tin's opening. Center the short piece on the long piece, sticky sides together. Place the strip across the top of the opening, leaving room for a scoop. Stick the tape ends to the sides of the tin.

matchbook

USE TO: Smooth a chipped nail. To fix it, run the jagged edge along the strike pad.

+ Direct a cab driver in an unfamiliar city. Carry the hotel's matchbook in your purse to jog your memory or to show to a driver who doesn't understand your language.

+ Make a travel sewing kit. Replace the matches with a needle or two and wrap a few colors of thread around the book.

◄ mayonnaise

USE TO: Condition hair at home. Starting at the scalp, comb ½ cup mayonnaise through strands and leave on for 15 minutes. Rinse thoroughly.

+ Erase water rings left on a tabletop during a cocktail party. Smear the full-fat spread onto the stain and let it sit for at least an hour, then wipe clean and buff.

+ Remove adhesive residue from bumper stickers or from any stickers on glass or mirrors.

melon baller

USE TO: Scoop out tomato seeds. The sharp-edged tool won't squash the flesh as much as a spoon does.

mesh strainer

USE TO: Crumble eggs. Push a hard-boiled egg through the mesh.

microwave

USE TO: Disinfect dirty sponges. Soak them in water spiked with white vinegar or lemon juice, then heat on high for one minute. Use an oven mitt when you remove them to avoid burning yourself.

+ Squeeze juice from lemons more easily. Place them in the microwave for 20 seconds first.

+ Decrystallize honey. Uncover the jar and warm at medium power for 30 seconds to a minute.

milk

USE TO: Turn freezer-case fillets into the catch of the (next) day. To help eliminate any frostbitten taste, submerge a frozen, unbreaded piece of fish in a broad, shallow bowl of milk, then refrigerate for 24 hours.
+ Cook up a moisturizing hair treatment. Add 1 teaspoon honey to 2 cups warm milk (use whole milk for coarse hair, skim for fine). Mix until the honey has dissolved and pour over dry hair. After 15 minutes, rinse with warm water, then shampoo and condition as usual.

milk carton

USE TO: Ship fragile trinkets. Insert bubble-wrapped breakables into a clean carton and pinch the top closed.

mini cooler

USE TO: Fake a perfectly timed meal. If side dishes (like corn on the cob) are ready before the main course, store them in an insulated case to retain their warmth.

mirror

USE TO: Create a dramatic centerpiece. Enlist an inexpensive closet-door mirror as a table runner. All along it, set vases of various heights and shapes (with and without flowers). Or use candles to create a glittering, romantic table.
+ Put a fireplace to work in summer. Stand a mirror inside it to reflect the soft, flickering light of pillar candles placed in front.

mitten ▶

USE TO: Deflect scratches to shades in your handbag. Slide them into a spare mitten.

money clip

USE TO: Streamline date-night essentials. Leave the bulky purse behind and slip cash, a credit card, and your driver's license into a clip, which fits neatly inside a slim clutch.

mouse pad

USE TO: Defend countertops against scald marks. Place a pad without a plastic coating under a hot pot as a trivet.

mouthwash bottle

USE TO: Soothe aches. Fill a flask-style bottle with hot tap water, then use it like a heating pad on sore muscles.

muffin pan

USE TO: Increase your baking capacity. An upside-down pan doubles as an extra cooling rack for sweet bonanzas.

muslin

USE TO: Preserve off-season clothing. Lining shelves or drawers with un-bleached, undyed, washed muslin keeps the acidity in the wood from damaging garments.

mustard powder

USE TO: Deodorize smelly glass jars. Wash them in a solution of 1 teaspoon powdered mustard to 1 quart warm water.

nail polish **to** nutcracker ▶

nail polish

USE TO: Color-code a crowded key ring. Differentiate sets for home and work with dabs of polish.
+ Rustproof a shaving-cream can. Coat the bottom rim with clear polish to shut out corrosive moisture and keep rust rings off your porcelain.
+ Seal an envelope. Apply a thin layer of clear polish when the flap just won't stay stuck.
+ Extend the life of jewelry. Paint a thin coat onto a costume piece to keep it from losing its luster.

nail-polish remover

USE TO: Loosen stubborn glue lids. Dip a cotton swab into remover and rub around the bottom of the cap.

+ Wipe away sticky bandage residue.
+ Clean ink stamps off your hands. Acetone-based remover will erase the evidence of a fun night out.

name tags ▶

USE TO: Make sure your brownie pan finds its way home from the potluck. Stick a label on the bottom.
+ Reunite all the look-alike long black coats with their proper owners at the end of a party. Place a pile of stickers in the coat room and have guests mark their outerwear.

+ Introduce the players at a wine-and-cheese party (HELLO, MY NAME IS MANCHEGO).
+ Serve as a unique mailing label.
+ Keep track of books that you lend out. Or make sure everyone at the book club goes home with her own copy of *Moby-Dick*.

napkin holder

USE TO: Organize bills on your desk.

newspaper

For this Master Multitasker's many uses, see page 96.

newspaper bag

USE TO: Sheathe a wet umbrella. When the weather report calls for storms, slip the plastic bag into your purse.

nonskid rug pad

USE TO: Make glasses stay put on a serving tray so breakfast in bed doesn't lead to mopping in your pajamas.
+ Stop pens and paper clips from rolling to the back of a desk drawer.
+ Prevent produce from bruising on the way home from the store. Laying a pad down in the car trunk keeps bags from shifting and tipping.

nutcracker

USE TO: Twist off a stuck cap. A cracker lends extra gripping power when you're dealing with stubborn tops of soda bottles.

MASTER MULTITASKER / NEWSPAPER / 1 Ripen tomatoes faster by wrapping each one in paper and leaving them out at room temperature. **2 To deodorize smelly food containers, seal balls of paper inside and let sit overnight. 3** Dry damp shoes and boots (and help them keep their shape) by stuffing them with crumpled paper. **4 Use newspaper to clean mirrors and windows. Spray on cleaning fluid and wipe streaks away. 5** To remove smudges on antique glass, dip paper in a solution of 1 part white vinegar and 1 part warm water, gently wipe the surface, and let air-dry. **6 Absorb odors in the refrigerator's vegetable drawer with a lining of newspaper. 7** To keep floors puddle-free in winter, keep a pile of newspapers by the entryway for slushy boots to rest on. **8 Save the comics section to wrap a child's birthday present, or use the wedding announcements for an engagement gift.**

oatmeal to oven rack ▶

oatmeal

USE TO: Clean a coffee grinder. Add a small amount to the grinder and run it until there's no longer an odor.

+ Clean hands after gardening. Scrub with a thick paste of oatmeal and water so the evidence of your green thumb will be seen in a vase, not under your fingernails.

+ Treat yourself to an at-home facial. Mix a packet of plain instant oatmeal with warm water and apply to skin. Let set for 5 to 10 minutes, then rinse well.

olive oil

For this Master Multitasker's many uses, see page 102.

onion ▶

USE TO: Clear the air in a dank basement. Cut an onion in half, place it on a plate, and leave it out overnight. Once the initial salad-bar aroma dissipates, you'll breathe easier.

orange

USE TO: Make a fragrant pomander to freshen a drawer or a closet. Stick cloves into an orange until it's completely covered. Roll it in a mixture of equal parts cinnamon, nutmeg, and orrisroot (or any other spices you like). Set it on wax paper until it's dry (two weeks or so), then cover it with cheesecloth or tissue paper.

+ Build snowmen without bundling up. For a holiday party, give each child three oranges, some toothpicks, a sturdy plate, and store-bought frosting. Use the frosting to glue the largest orange to the plate. Poke a few toothpicks halfway into the top of the fruit and stick a smaller orange onto them. Repeat with the third orange, and top it off with a (frosting-glued) hat made from a vanilla wafer and a peppermint candy. Use candy-cane pieces for arms and a nose, cloves for the eyes, and a red licorice string for a scarf.

oven mitt

USE TO: Store hot hair-styling tools safely in a drawer or a suitcase when you can't wait for them to cool.

+ Cushion electronic gadgets and other fragile items when you're packing for a trip.

+ Minimize flesh wounds when you hold a squirming kitten to administer medicine—or whatever else causes the claws to come out.

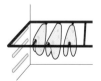

oven rack

USE TO: Make healthier crisp taco shells. Drape flour tortillas over the bars of an oven rack so they form inverted U-shapes. Bake at 350° F for about 10 minutes, or until they harden. Use tongs to remove.

MASTER MULTITASKER / OLIVE OIL / 1 Make a fume-free polish for wood furniture by mixing 3 parts olive oil and 1 part distilled white vinegar. (Test on a small area before going to town.) **2 Moisturize cuticles by applying a small amount of oil to the nail beds. 3** Rub on a thin layer after showering or waxing to hydrate skin. **4 To remove makeup dregs under the eyes, dab on olive oil and wipe off with a wet washcloth. 5** Buff streaks out of stainless steel with a little oil on a terry-cloth rag, then shine with a dry paper towel. (Some cleaners, like ammonia, can dull steel.) **6 To prevent hair balls, add ¹/₈ to ¹/₄ teaspoon olive oil to cat food. 7** Silence noisy doors by applying a bit of oil to the squeaky hinges. **8 Unstick a stuck zipper by running a cotton swab with a drop of oil over the teeth. 9** Get a closer shave by using olive oil instead of shaving cream.

packing tape to pumice stone ▶

packing tape

USE TO: Limit the collateral damage of a toppled vase. Gently press tape over the broken glass to pick up the shards.
+ Remove a shallow splinter. Press the sticky side onto it and it should lift off with the tape.

paint-sample strips

USE TO: Make place cards that will flatter dinner guests. Choose a strip with a shade that suggests each person's distinctive quality (like Inner Glow or Delicate Peach). Write her name on it, fold the strip, and prop it up by her plate.

+ Label a present. Punch a hole in a strip and use as a colorful gift tag.

painter's tape

USE TO: Seal and reseal family-size packages of cereal and snack foods.

pant hanger

USE TO: Straighten a rolled poster. Suspend it from one pant hanger and use another to weigh down the bottom.
+ Air-dry a damp bath mat.

+ Store place mats, runners, and napkins crease-free.
+ Steam a wrinkled garment the easy way. Place it on a hanger, clip a pant hanger to the bottom to hold the garment taut, and hang the whole thing in the bathroom while you shower.
+ Organize sheets of gift wrap and tissue paper in a spare closet.

paper clip

USE TO: Secure pleats while you iron. Attach a clip to the bottom of each fold.
+ Mark your page in a book.
+ Sub for a lost zipper pull.
+ Hang a holiday ornament.

paper-clip dispenser

USE TO: Hold bobby pins on your vanity.

paper plates ▶

USE TO: Keep china from chipping. Layer paper plates between each piece of the good stuff.

paper shredder

USE TO: Dress up presents. Shred tissue paper to use as filler in gift bags and boxes.
+ Recycle discarded holiday gift wrap. Instead of trashing it, shred it to cushion decorations until next year.

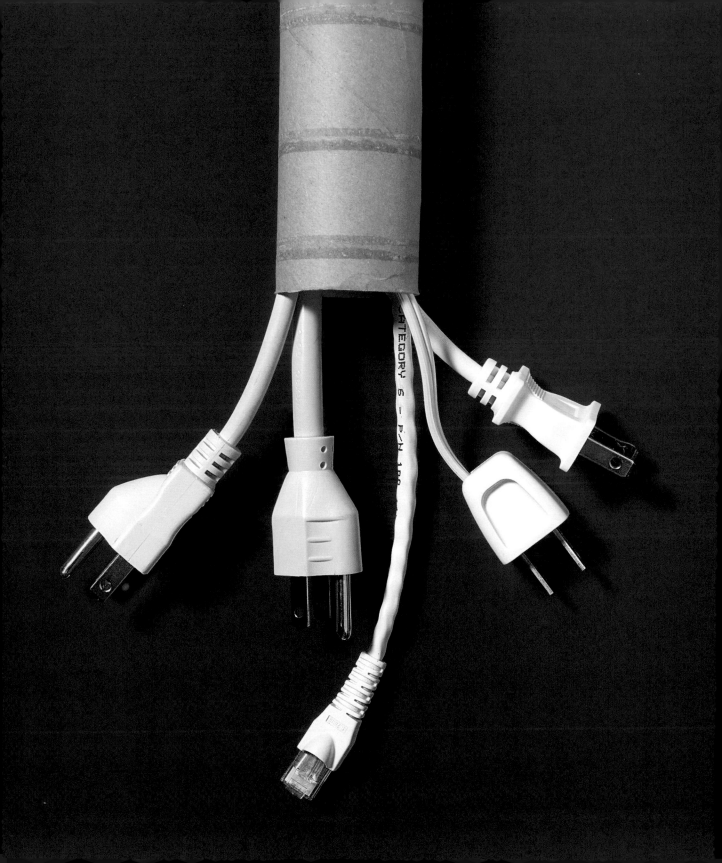

◄ paper-towel tube

USE TO: Tame a tangle of computer cables.
+ Ward off wrinkles in a silk scarf. Wrap it around a tube between wearings.
+ Dispense plastic bags. Stuff them in a tube (stashed in a drawer) and pull out as needed.
+ Make Lincoln Logs. Cut a square hole roughly the dimension of a tube in each end of several tubes. Tuck tubes perpendicularly into the holes to build a structure.
+ Preserve remnants of gift wrap. Wind them around the tube and fasten with a rubber band—or just roll them and slide them into the tube.

parchment paper

USE TO: Give cupcakes or muffins a bit of professional polish for the next bake sale. Instead of using liners, place generously sized squares of paper in a muffin tin's greased cups, press down and fold gathers neatly, then fill cups with batter.

pasta maker

USE TO: Shred paper once you've given up the fantasy of making your own linguine (since shredding may wear down the machine's blades).

pastry blender

USE TO: Break up leftover cooked sausage or ground beef before adding to spaghetti sauce or chili.

pastry tip

USE TO: Prevent diamonds from going down the drain. Stand a tip next to the sink to hold your ring while you wash up.
+ Set a sweet table. Spray-paint leaf or scalloped pastry tips in fun colors to serve as place-card holders.

pencil

USE TO: Steam ruffles and other frills in silk or synthetic fabrics without scorching your fingers. Roll tissue paper or a strip of white cotton around the pencil base and secure it with tape. Then use the tool to raise the ruffles and straighten them out as you steam.

+ Loosen a stuck zipper. A little lead rubbed across both sides of the teeth does the trick.

pencil eraser

USE TO: Keep artwork from scratching the wall. Cut the erasers from a pair of pencils and glue them to the bottom corners of a frame so it doesn't wobble and bang.
+ Substitute for a lost earring back. Slice off a new, clean pencil eraser and pop it onto the post until you get home.

penny

For this Master Multitasker's many uses, see page 116.

peppermint tin ▶

USE TO: Carry crayons for sketching sessions with your favorite up-and-coming artist when inspiration (or boredom) strikes.
+ Hold tissues on the go. Fold a pack inside the tin to keep them dry and intact in your purse or beach bag.

permanent marker

USE TO: Cover bleach spots on an otherwise solid-black garment.
+ Conceal light scuffs on dark shoes.
+ Tone down red eyes in photographs. A fine-tipped marker gets the devil out.

+ Decorate Halloween pumpkins without the danger or the mess. Instead of cutting out spooky designs, draw them on.

petroleum jelly

USE TO: Prevent a nail-polish cap from sticking. Dab the jelly around the bottle's ridges before sealing.
+ Quiet squeaky doors. Apply jelly to the hinges.
+ Make eyelashes glisten. Dot a bit on with a fingertip.

pewter tray

USE TO: Create a signature wedding keepsake. Rent an engraving pen from a hardware store and ask guests to sign their names on the platter.

photo album

USE TO: File frequently used business cards. Slide a card in each slot of a brag book for a purse-ready Rolodex.
+ Stash fabric swatches and paint chips so at least one area of your home renovation is under control.

photo box

USE TO: Organize delicate jewelry. Store chains, charms, and small earrings in individual vellum envelopes inside the box.

photo corners

USE TO: Frame and tack down a plain-paper gift tag.

photo tree

USE TO: Orchestrate a multicourse meal. Display all the recipes you need on a stand so you don't miss a beat (or an ingredient) as you work.

photograph

USE TO: Play a game of Concentration. Print doubles of your favorite photos, turn them upside down, mix them up, and commence with the flipping.

pillowcase

USE TO: Craft a child's play smock. Cut a hole for the neck from the fold and two armholes in the sides. Gather the fabric between the neck and each armhole and tie with ribbon.

+ Dustproof a party dress. Slit a hole in the top of the case and slide it over a hanger.

+ Store a set of linens together.

+ Shield a sewing machine or some other small appliance from crevice-seeking dust.

+ Organize lingerie in a suitcase.

+ Avoid a dust storm when cleaning a ceiling fan. Slip an old pillowcase over each blade, then pull the fabric back to lift the dirt and catch it in the case.

pitcher

USE TO: Keep cooking utensils (ladles, spatulas, tongs) or office tools (ruler, scissors) at your fingertips.

+ Display a casual bouquet.

+ Make a space-saving vertical bread basket for baguettes.

+ Shave time off the table-setting process. Place silverware and napkins in a large pitcher for guests to grab.

pizza slicer

USE TO: Chop a salad. Fill a bowl with lettuce and toppings, then run the slicer through it all.

place mat

USE TO: Prevent water rings. Using pinking shears, cut a mat into squares for coasters.

+ Surf the Internet. Recycle a plastic mat as a mouse pad.

planter

USE TO: Serve as a side table, topped with a piece of glass.

◄ plastic bags

USE TO: Put a paint job on hold. When you've finished for the day, wrap your brush in a bag and secure it with a rubber band. (This will keep it moist for a day or so.)

+ Cushion your knees (and keep them dry) when gardening. Tie a few bags around each knee before settling down to pull weeds.

+ Cut down on countertop mess. Peel vegetables and fruits into a plastic bag, then toss.

+ Hold a wet umbrella so it doesn't soak your purse.

+ Protect a cookbook. Wrap everything but the page you're working with in plastic.

+ Adapt a planter to fit a short shrub. Crumple bags to fill the bottom of a too-deep pot. (Be sure not to cover the drainage hole.)

plastic cup ▶

USE TO: Make a party lantern. Cut X's into the bottoms of small cups, then push the bulbs from a string of holiday lights through the holes. Hang the string from a doorway or a window.

plastic trays

USE TO: Contain rain-boot runoff. Place a tray near each entryway when wet weather descends.

plastic wrap

USE TO: Carry unwieldy packages. Twist several feet of wrap into a sturdy rope, tie it around a box, and knot the rest to form a handle.

+ Store china sets. Cover each piece in plastic, then wrap up the whole stack.
+ Keep leaky toiletries from putting a damper on your next vacation. Unscrew the cap, cover the opening and the neck with wrap, and screw the cap back on. If the top loosens, the liquid is less likely to ooze.

Play-Doh

USE TO: Prevent burned fingers on the Fourth of July. Holding a sparkler in a can of "clay" protects your hand from sparks as it burns down.

popcorn

USE TO: Cushion a care package. Fill the empty space in the box with plain air-popped corn.

Post-it Notes

USE TO: Clean a keyboard. Slide the sticky side through the crevices to collect dust, debris, and crumbs.
+ Find your way on the road. Jot directions on a note and stick it to the steering wheel for an ultra-low-tech form of GPS.
+ Serve as folder tabs to divide a stack of papers into sections.

potato

USE TO: Remove soft cheese and other sticky food remnants from a grater. Cut the potato in half and rub it across both sides of the tool.

potpourri wax tart

USE TO: Freshen a smelly car. Pop one of these tarts (which are used in fragrance burners) into a cup holder.

puffy paint

USE TO: Roam the house with no fear of slipping. Dot some on the soles of socks and let dry before taking them for a spin.

pumice stone

USE TO: Depill a favorite, well-worn cardigan. Lightly run the stone across the surface.

MASTER MULTITASKER / PENNY / 1 Prevent algae from growing in a birdbath by tossing a few pre-1982 coins into the water. The copper keeps the organisms from multiplying. **2 To check the wear on a tire, insert a penny into a groove with Lincoln's head pointing into the tire; if you can clearly see his whole head, it's time to invest in new wheels. 3** Stabilize a wobbly table with a cent slid under the too-short leg. (It looks much tidier than a stack of sugar packets.) **4 Use a penny to replace a missing piece of a board game. But no fighting over who gets to be president! 5** If you can't find a screwdriver to open an electronic gadget's battery pack, try the edge of a penny. **6 To make an impromptu percussion instrument on a desperate rainy day, place pennies in a foil pie pan, cover it with another pan, and tape the edges together. 7** Glue coins to the soles of an old pair of your child's shoes for a no-commitment tap-dancing tryout.

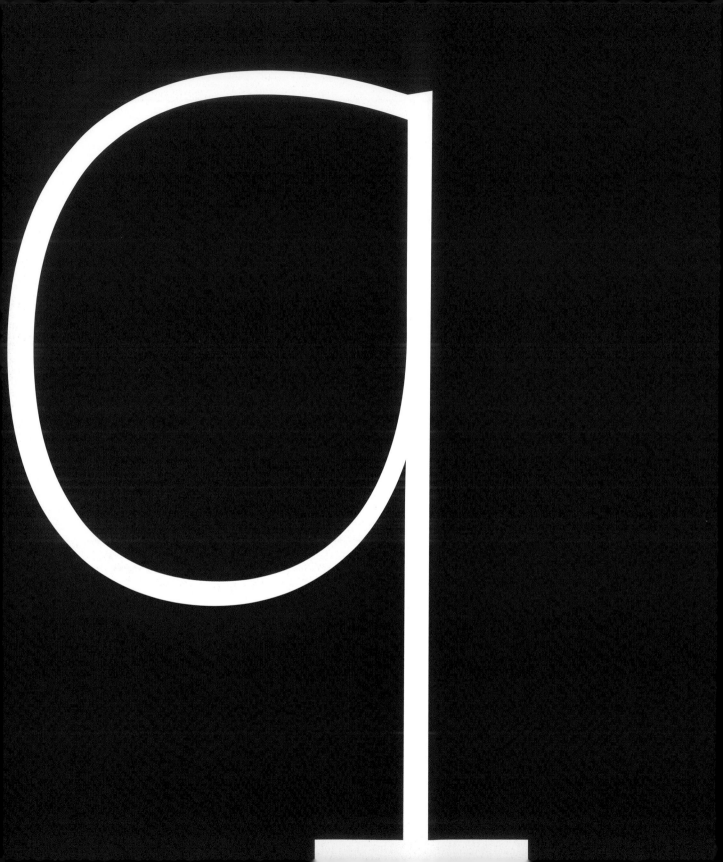

Q-tips to quilt ▶

Q-tips ▶

USE TO: Make a quickie cosmetics kit for a tiny evening bag. Dip cotton swabs into eye shadow, concealer, and lip gloss. Roll them up in a plastic bag and go.
+ Polish crevices in silver pieces.
+ Extend the life of batteries in a cordless phone, cell phone, or laptop. Clean the battery contacts with a swab dipped in alcohol.
+ Touch up paint in tight corners, or apply stain in the ridges of architectural details.

+ Artfully dab on Halloween-costume makeup. (Save your brushes for the good stuff.)
+ Clean the computer. Swipe a swab through open spaces in a keyboard to clear out dust and crumbs.

quarter

USE TO: Play an icebreaker game. Hand out a coin to each guest at a party. Everyone must then share a personal story that happened during the year on that coin. If it predates the person, she can invent a story—the more elaborate, the better—or riff on a historical event.
+ Make a quick measurement. A quarter is almost one (0.955) inch in diameter.

quiche pan

USE TO: Display a child's drawing or painting proudly on the refrigerator. To make a kitchen-appropriate frame, remove the center insert from the pan (also known as a fluted tart pan) and attach magnets to the back of the rim.
+ Give a piecrust a fluted edge. Roll the sides of the pan around the dough's edge to make a uniform pattern.

+ Cool freshly baked brownies faster. Remove the center of the pan and upend the rest to use as a cooling rack.

quilt

USE TO: Turn a barebones bed into a focal point. Wrap a quilt around an old headboard and staple the back. Or hang a curtain rod a few feet above the bed and drape the quilt over it. Besides warming a bland room, the quilt provides padding for bedtime-reading comfort.

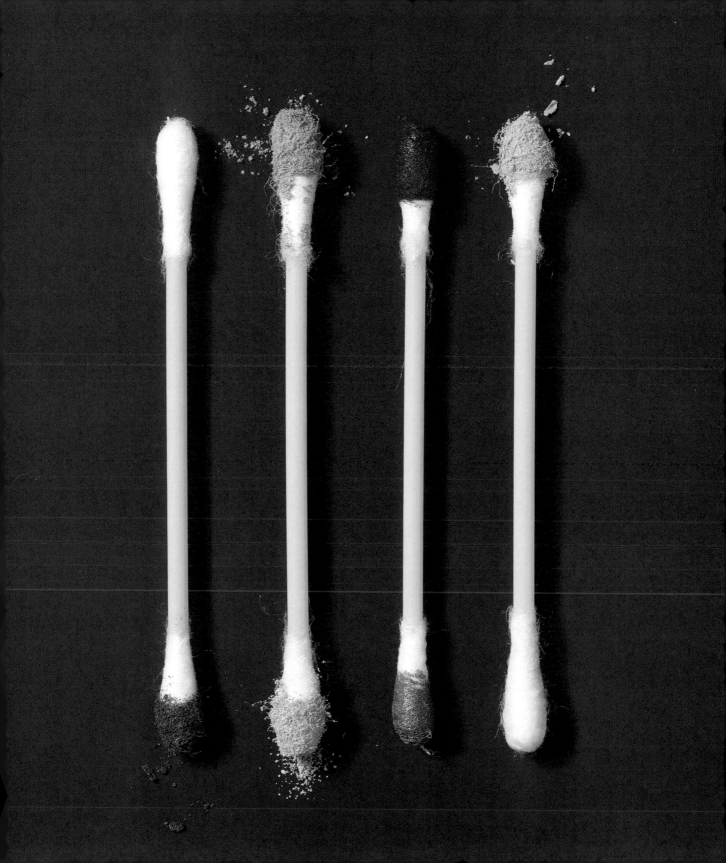

rain boot to **rubbing alcohol** ▶

rain boot

USE TO: Chill beverages for a party. Fill waterproof Wellies with cubes (removing any inserts first) and pop in bottles of wine, bubbly, vodka, or soda.

+ Contain soaking-wet umbrellas post-downpour.

+ Round up kids' desk or art supplies. Use an outgrown or orphaned little boot as a funky holder for pencils and rulers.

+ Keep a child's Golden Books from tumbling off the shelves. Put last year's boots back to work as bookends: Fill spare socks with rice, tie them with rubber bands, and drop them into the boots.

raisin ▶

USE TO: Restore bubbles to Champagne. Drop a raisin (or three) into near-flat sparkling wine. Any last gasps of carbon dioxide will stick to the raisin, then be released in a few minutes as tiny bubbles.

red ornament

USE TO: Banish birds from your beloved tomato plants. Fake out the flock by hanging red ornaments where fruit will eventually hang. When it does, the birds will leave it alone, since they have already (fruitlessly) pecked at the ornaments.

ribbon

USE TO: Hang a shower curtain in place of plain plastic rings.

+ Upgrade a basic drugstore gift bag. Replace the sad, stringy handles with colorful ribbon run through the existing holes.

+ Update an old lamp shade. Attach strips of grosgrain ribbon to the top and bottom edges of the shade with a thin layer of Elmer's or fabric glue.

rice

USE TO: Clean your coffee grinder. Mill a handful of uncooked white rice. The fine particles will absorb stale odors and clean out residual grounds and oil.

+ Prepare a stained vase for a new batch of blooms. If you can't reach the residue at the bottom, add a tablespoon of rice and a lot of warm, soapy water, shake, and rinse. Repeat until clean.

rice cooker

USE TO: Steam hot towels for an at-home spa experience. Wet and wring out washcloths, fold in thirds, roll up, and steam in the cooker for about five minutes. (Transfer towels with tongs—they're hot!—to a plate to cool a bit.)

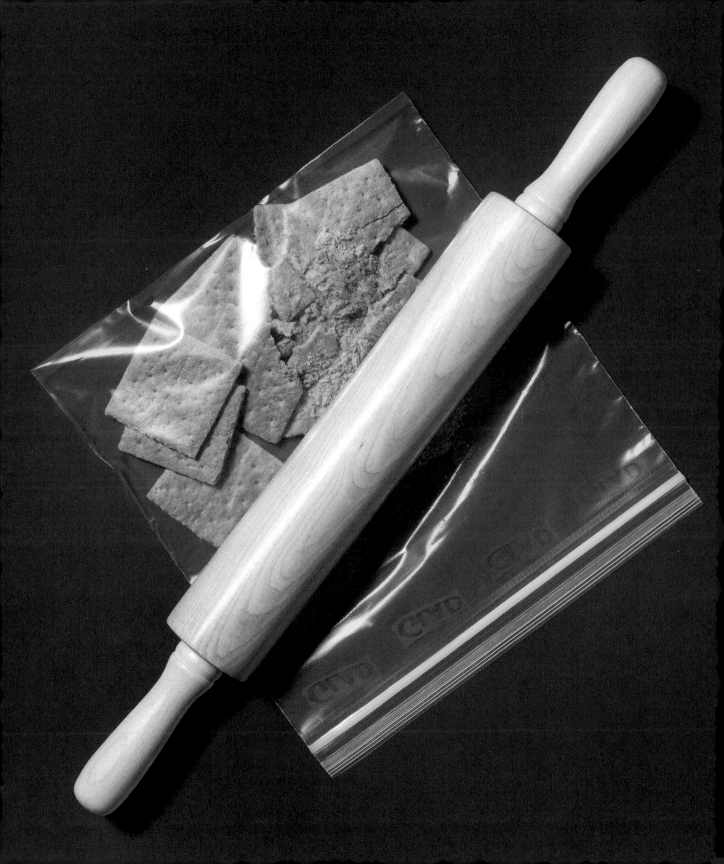

rocks

USE TO: Keep books straight on a shelf. Ground your reading collection by enlisting large, smooth rocks as bookends.

+ Insulate a potted plant. A layer of decorative pebbles on top of the soil helps keep it from drying out.

+ Create an artfully rustic tic-tac-toe game you won't mind leaving out on the table. Paint X's and O's on small stones and draw a grid on any square surface (a chalkboard, an old serving platter).

+ Construct an outdoorsy coatrack. Attach rocks to flat wooden drawer pulls with a polyurethane-based glue (like Gorilla Glue). Screw the knobs into a wood plank and mount it at eye level on an entry way wall.

◄ rolling pin

USE TO: Crush nuts or crackers. Place the food in a plastic bag, seal it, then roll the pin over it.

+ Massage your arches. Roll your feet over it from ball to heel and back again.

rolling suitcase

USE TO: Store currently unneeded seasonal items, from summer clothes to holiday table linens.

rubber band

For this Master Multitasker's many uses, see page 128.

rubbing alcohol

USE TO: Remove permanent marker from countertops and walls. Dampen a cotton ball or a soft cloth with alcohol and scour the spot. (Test on a hidden area first.)

+ Fix self-tanner mistakes. Use a little alcohol to remove it from places you didn't mean it to go.

+ Improvise a soft gel pack to soothe aches or keep kids' lunches cold. Mix 1 part rubbing alcohol with 3 parts water and freeze in a freezer-safe zippered plastic bag.

+ Remove hairspray residue from bathroom walls. Onto vinyl wallpaper or semigloss (not flat) paint, spray a mixture of 1 part rubbing alcohol, 2 parts water, and a dash of dishwashing liquid. Wipe clean.

MASTER MULTITASKER / RUBBER BAND / 1 Create traction at the ends of a hanger (so camisole straps and slippery dresses stay put) by wrapping the outer corners with rubber bands. **2 Use them to secure wayward glasses in the dishwasher, tethering them to the prongs.** **3**To add a unique touch to a gift in a snap, stretch several colored bands around it instead of adding a ho-hum bow. Bonus: You can slip a card under the bands. **4 Give a pregnant belly a bit more breathing room in pants by looping a rubber band through the buttonhole, then securing both ends around the button.** **5**Create patterns on Easter eggs by positioning bands around them before dipping them in dye. **6 Slip a few around a cup at different heights to help a klutzy kid get a better grip on his glass of milk.** **7**Get a handle on a hard-to-budge jar lid by encircling it with a rubber band.

salad spinner to Swiffer ▶

salad spinner

USE TO: Dry your favorite cashmere sweater after hand washing. To cut the (endless!) time in half, use a large spinner with a pull cord to shake off excess water, then lay flat to dry.
+ Distribute salad dressing evenly— or undo a vinaigrette overdose— with a gentle spin.
+ Cover a cake outdoors to keep it safe from flies.

salt

For this Master Multitasker's many uses, see page 142.

salt and pepper shakers

USE TO: Sub as bud vases on a bathroom vanity or a night table.

sand

USE TO: Catch candle drippings. Place a layer of sand under a pillar or votive candle. When it burns down, the wax is tossed out with the sand instead of sticking to the holder.

sandpaper ▶

USE TO: Sharpen dull scissors. A few snips will help to maintain their edge.

saucer

USE TO: Dish out decorative soap. A pretty saucer adds a refined touch to a guest bath.

scissors

USE TO: Neatly chop canned tomatoes.
+ Divvy up a pizza.

seam ripper

USE TO: Tear into plastic-wrapped CDs and DVDs without wrecking your nails.
+ Cut away lint and hair from a vacuum's roller brush.
+ Remove rough, itchy tags from scarves and shirts.

sheet pan

USE TO: Safeguard stationery and special-occasion cards. Store them in a covered sheet pan to keep the paper's edges crisp and the cards pristine while awaiting their big moment.

shell

USE TO: Dish out salt—and bring a touch of the seashore to your table settings.
+ Grow diminutive plants, such as succulents, which don't require lots of water.

shoe bag

USE TO: Cushion copper pots to avoid scratches. Store them safely in soft pouches.

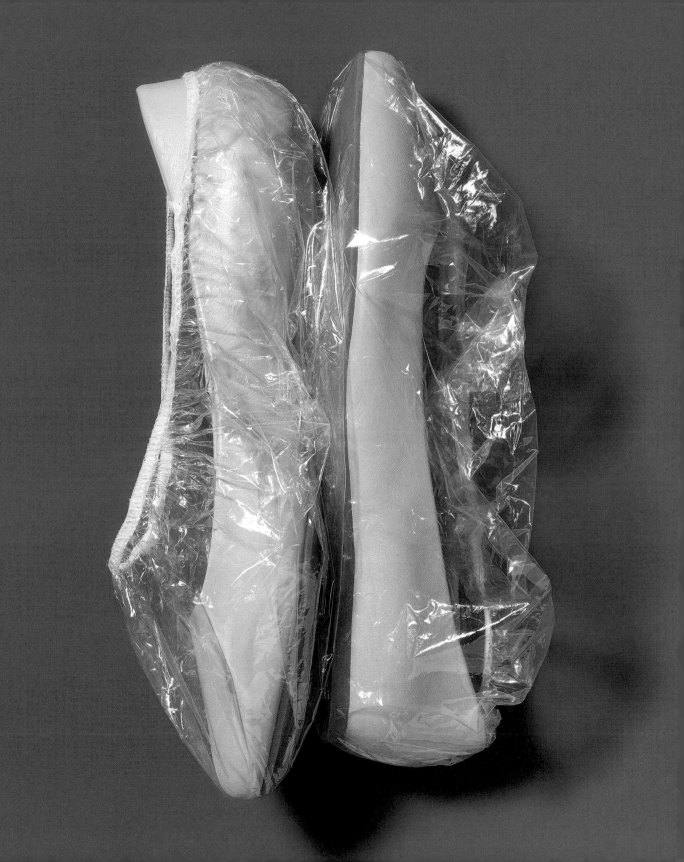

shoe box

USE TO: Store old bills and documents. Give unattractive filing cabinets the boot and replace them with shoe boxes covered in decorative paper.

+ Tidy holiday lights. Cut off the edges of a box lid, wrap a string of lights around it to keep the strand from tangling, and store the whole thing in the box.

shoe organizer

USE TO: Gather all your supplies for gift wrapping—scissors, tape, bows, tags—in one handy place.

+ Contain and control your spice collection. To keep the bay leaves from knocking over the oregano on cupboard shelves, hang a clear organizer on the pantry door and pop in the spices.

+ Set up a home bar. Slip wine and liquor bottles into the pockets, along with a cocktail shaker, stirrers, and bar towels.

+ Construct a child's arts-and-crafts tool belt. Cut off one pocketed strip and sew a ribbon onto each end.

+ Store panty hose and tights. To simplify your morning routine, keep hose in a clear organizer with pockets labeled for black, navy, sheer, and opaque versions.

+ Stash soaps, razors, sprays, and other bathroom essentials.

shoe polish

USE TO: Spruce up wood furniture and fill in scratches. Apply a pea-size dot of wax polish in a compatible shade, then buff with a soft cotton cloth.

shower caddy

USE TO: Store laundry supplies. You'll know right where to find them *and* when it's time to stock up.

◄ shower cap

USE TO: Keep the clothes in your suitcase protected from dirt on shoes.

shower-curtain liner

USE TO: Convert a dining-room table into a craft station that's paint- and markerproof.

+ Do dew diligence. Place a liner under a picnic blanket to shield it from mud and grass stains, and protect picnickers' bottoms from soggy ground.

shower-curtain rings

USE TO: Keep scarves or purses sorted (and off the closet floor). Place curtain rings on a rod and thread scarves through them, or hook handbag straps to them.

silicone cutting mat

USE TO: Stop crying over spilled milk. Instead of a place mat, try a nonslip silicone mat under your child's cereal bowl.
+ Anchor a slip-prone rug.
+ Slip between breakable dishes to cushion them during a move.

silverware

USE TO: Make hangers for lightweight items, like aprons and pot holders. To put lovely but languishing utensils to practical use, bore a small hole into each handle with a titanium drill bit, bend the end of the piece into a U-shape (warming the metal with a hair dryer will help), then nail the hook to the wall.

six-pack container

USE TO: Cart the flatware and condiments to a backyard barbecue.
+ Create a (minor) emergency kit for the family car. Include wet wipes, tissues, granola bars, a lint roller, and other sanity-saving necessities.

skateboard

USE TO: Build a rad display shelf for a kid's collectibles. Screw a pair of L-brackets (a little more than half as long as the board's width) into two wall studs about 16 inches apart. Remove the board's trucks and wheels (or leave them on if they aren't grungy and you want to hide the supports). Center the board on the brackets and attach with screws.

+ Save your back some bending when you paint. Use the board to slide the paint can along with you as you go.

Slinky

USE TO: Make a desk organizer that turns back into a toy when you're bored. Slip notes between rings, or link ends and gather pens in the middle.

soap ▶

USE TO: Take the grit out of gardening. Scrape your nails along a bar so the soap gets under them and keeps everything else out.

+ Facilitate smooth exits from a door that sticks. Run a bar of soap over the top for clean getaways.
+ Unstick furniture drawers. Rub a bar along the tracks.
+ Loosen a stuck zipper. Slide a bar along the teeth.
+ Mark a hem. No dressmaker's chalk on hand? Use that last sliver of soap.
+ Get rid of aphids and other pests on plants. Make a homemade spray by mixing a solution of 5 to 10 drops of mild liquid soap and 1 gallon of water. Add a few drops of cooking oil so the solution will stick to the plants.

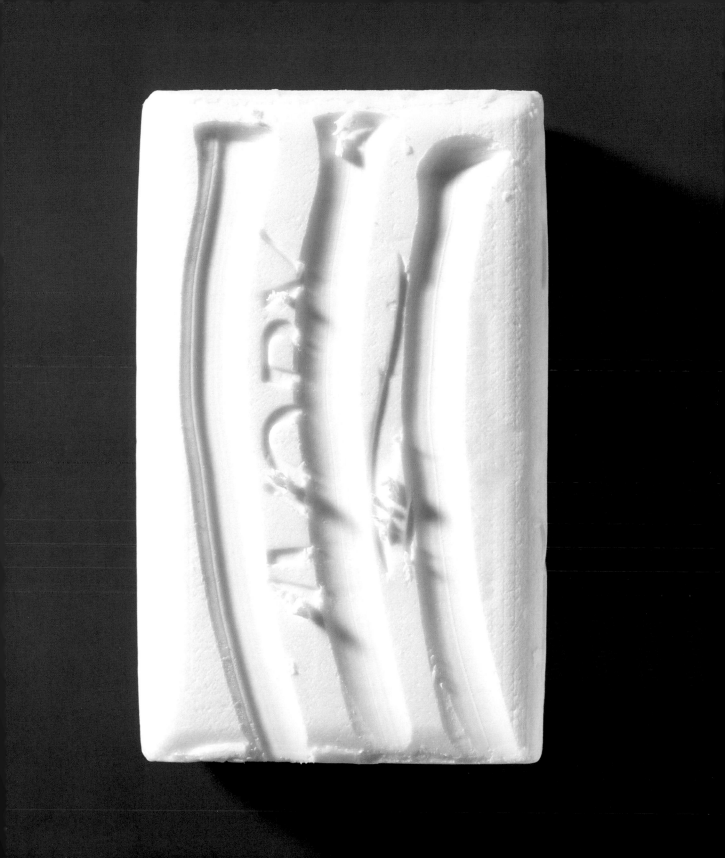

soap case

USE TO: Shield a compact camera from scratches. Tuck it into a hard-sided travel case.

soccer net

USE TO: Score with your all-star by making a sporty headboard. Attach a net (39 inches for a twin bed, 54 for a full) to the wall behind the bed with Velcro.

soda bottle

USE TO: Help your old (non-high-efficiency) toilet go green. Set a water-filled plastic bottle in the tank to reduce the volume needed to refill it with each flush.
+ Pour seed into a bird feeder. Cut a bottle in half and use the top part as a funnel.

+ Prop up a boot. A bottle in each leg will keep your favorite pair in shape.

soup tureen

USE TO: Chill wine when stew season is over.
+ Hold potpourri near an entryway for a pretty, fragrant welcome.
+ Build an emergency cookie-baking kit. Stash essentials, like cutters, sprinkles, and tubes of icing, under the lid.
+ Arrange an easy centerpiece. Float showy flowers on the surface or stack citrus fruits inside.
+ Hold a small potted plant. Set it atop a layer of pebbles for drainage.

◄ spaghetti

USE TO: Light candles. One stick of pasta can fire up a whole birthday cake's worth of wicks.
+ Mark a page in a cookbook.
+ Spear a cold hors d'oeuvre.
+ Test whether a cake is fully baked.
+ Preserve a top-notch frosting job in transit. Poke a few pieces of spaghetti into the top and sides of your creation before wrapping it.

sponge

USE TO: Sweep pet hair from upholstery or clothing. Run a damp sponge across the fabric.
+ Soothe a fevered brow. Dampen a sponge and put it in the freezer briefly to use as a cold compress.

+ Keep soil from escaping a planter. Cut a piece of sponge slightly larger than the drainage hole to cover it with before filling the pot.
+ Save energy. In summer, keep hot air out of the house by using sponges to plug gaps between the air conditioner and the window.
+ Buffer your wall when removing a nail. Place a sponge between the wall and the hammer to prevent scratches.
+ Pull off a perfect pedicure. Wedge the pieces of a cut-up sponge between your toes before painting on polish.

spring

USE TO: Show off mementos. Slide photos and other souvenirs between the coils.
+ Neatly store the week's mail until you get around to, *ugh,* the utility bill, the doctor's invoice, the umpteenth 0 percent APR credit-card offer…

starch

USE TO: Keep canvas or nylon sneakers clean. To repel dirt and grime, spray a light coat of starch on the inside and outside of white kicks before wearing.

Static Guard

USE TO: Fight fly-aways. Spray brush bristles from about two feet away, let dry, then brush and style hair as usual.

step stool

USE TO: Rest your soles. Store shoes on the tiers of a stool in the closet.

storybook pages

USE TO: Add some character(s) to a table setting. Get kids' attention at mealtime by sandwiching some of their favorite book pages between lamination sheets (sold at office-supply stores) to use as place mats.

straw ▶

USE TO: Core a strawberry.
+ Boost a bouquet to new heights. Insert the bottom of each stem into a straw to make it fit a tall (opaque) vase.

Styrofoam peanuts

USE TO: Supplement potting mix. To lighten a planter and improve drainage, cover the bottom with a layer of packing peanuts before adding soil.

sugar

USE TO: Smooth dry, peeling lips. With a toothbrush, gently rub a paste of sugar and petroleum jelly back and forth until the roughness is gone.
+ Cut grease on hands. Give them a good rub with moistened sugar.
+ Scale back the spiciness in food. If you put too much chili or hot pepper in a dish, stir in a bit of sugar to temper the burn.

sugar bowl

USE TO: Keep tabs on your keys. Place an unused bowl by the front door and drop your keys in it when you come home.

sunscreen

USE TO: Fill in for shaving lotion. (Expired sunscreen will do the trick.)

Swiffer

USE TO: Spiff up those leather shoes buried at the back of the closet. Wipe them with a dry cloth to remove accumulated dust and dirt.

MASTER MULTITASKER / SALT / 1 Remove coffee and tea stains from cups by rubbing them with a salted lemon peel. **2 Make polishing silver easier by massaging salt into the tarnished areas before cleaning. 3** To lift red-wine stains from washables, stretch the fabric over a bowl, cover the stain with salt, then carefully pour boiling water over it. **4 Clean dirt from leafy vegetables by washing them in a bath of salt water. 5** To chill a bottle of bubbly fast, put it in a bucket, place ice around the base, and sprinkle with a few table-spoons of salt. Layer ice and salt until they reach the neck. Fill the bucket with water, wait 10 minutes, and serve. **6 Sprinkle a handful of salt over a broken egg to make cleanup easier. 7** To prevent frost from accu-mulating on the insides of car windows, rub them with a solution of 2 teaspoons salt to 1 gallon hot water. Wipe dry. **8 Pour a solution of ½ cup salt to 1 quart hot water down a drain to clean it.**

tablecloth to Twister mat ▶

tablecloth

USE TO: Reupholster a worn seat cushion. Remove the seat and place it upside down on the wrong side of the cloth, avoiding any stained sections. Cut around the seat, leaving a three-inch border on all sides. Fold the fabric over, as if wrapping a present, and attach it to the bottom of the seat with a staple gun (place staples an inch apart). Then pop the seat back onto the chair.

tackle box

USE TO: Make fishing for sewing supplies easier. Stash pins, thread, and needles in the top compartments and scissors, rulers, and larger notions below.

talcum powder

USE TO: Hush up squeaky floors. For a temporary fix, sprinkle powder on the noisy area and sweep it into the cracks. (Be sure to remove any traces of powder should you decide to refinish the floor.)

tea

USE TO: Restore the gleam to rusty garden tools. Brew a few pots of strong black tea. When it's cool, pour it into a bucket and soak the tools for a few hours before wiping clean. (Wear rubber gloves so your hands don't get stained.)

tea bag

USE TO: Soothe mosquito bites. Place a cold, brewed bag on a sting and let sit for 5 minutes.
+ Subtly scent a drawer. Place a lavender, vanilla, or mint tea bag in with delicates instead of a sachet.

tea strainer

USE TO: Decorate baked goods. Fill the basket with confectioners' sugar and lightly tap over brownies or lemon bars for a sweet finish.

teapot ▶

USE TO: Pump up your pancake presentation. Pour syrup from a small teapot instead of a plastic bottle the next time you treat someone to breakfast in bed.

tennis ball

For this Master Multitasker's many uses, see page 154.

tension rod

USE TO: Keep pot lids from rattling around in a drawer. Position a short tension rod a quarter of the way in as a divider. Stack pans in the larger section, and lean lids against the rod on the other side.

tie rack

USE TO: Hang pot holders and towels.
+ Organize necklaces—by length, color, and so on.
+ Keep scarves off the floor.
+ Sort mail. Place a wood rack flat on a desk or a countertop and stick in the paperwork.

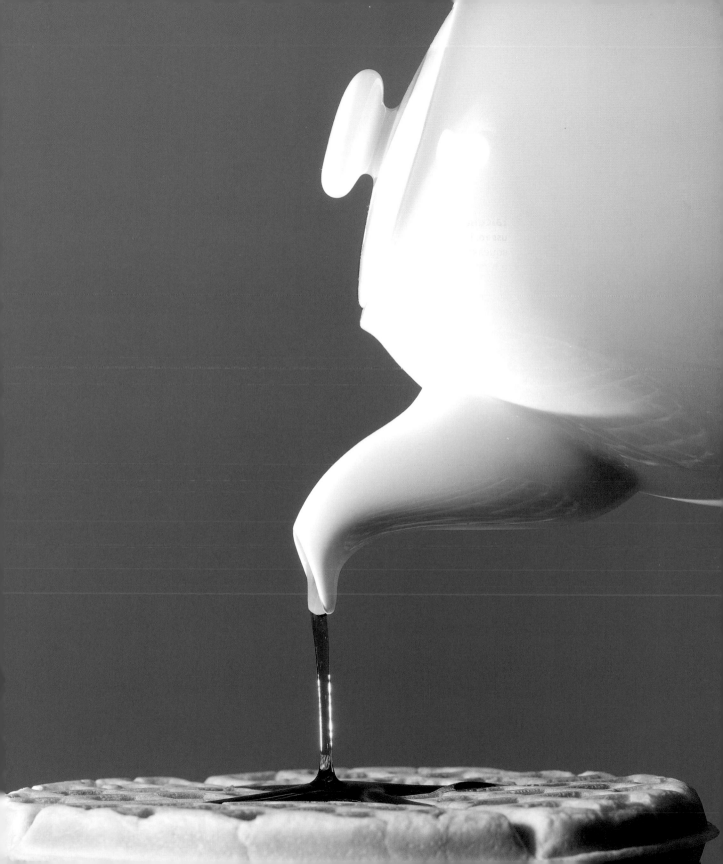

tissue box

USE TO: Dispense plastic grocery bags. Stuff them into an empty box, then pull one out whenever you need it.

tissue paper

USE TO: Avoid ironing while on the road. Pack shirts and blouses between layers of tissue paper and they'll arrive wrinkle-free.

+ Help a purse and boots keep their shape. Tissue stuffed inside prevents premature wilting.

toilet-paper tube

USE TO: Store hair accessories. Clip bobby pins to a tube or stretch wrapped elastics around it so you don't have to go searching for them under couch cushions or in the depths of your purse.

+ Store an extension cord. Loop it around your hand, then slide the cord into a tube.

◄ toothbrush

USE TO: Find the business end of plastic wrap. Rub a brush around the roll to locate that elusive edge.

+ Remove silk from an ear of corn.

+ Clean hard-to-get-at areas around faucets and other fixtures.

+ Scour bathroom tiles. (An electric toothbrush will save elbow grease.)

+ Groom unruly eyebrows. A hard-bristled brush does the trick.

+ Salvage a stained garment. Brush in a prewash spot treatment.

toothbrush holder

USE TO: Display blossoms. Fill a holder with water and place a stem in each hole for a foolproof, evenly spaced arrangement. Full-flowered types, like peonies and ranunculus, work best.

toothpaste (standard)

USE TO: Restore a damaged CD. With a cotton pad, rub a dot of a standard paste (not a gel, tartar-control, or whitening formula) in a straight line from the center of the CD outward, covering scratches. Rinse well.

+ Shine chrome (dab on, buff off) and tarnished silver (rub on, rinse, buff) and piano keys (rub on carefully with a damp cotton swab, wipe dry, buff).

+ Diminish scratches on acrylic accessories (work in with a toothbrush, wipe off) and scuffs on linoleum (scrub on, wipe off).

+ Clean mineral deposits from a steam iron's soleplate (dab on, rub in, wipe off).

toothpick ▶

USE TO: Keep plastic wrap from smooshing a birthday cake's icing. Stick toothpicks in the top before covering.
+ Hold a button away from fabric to keep from sewing it on too tightly.
+ Press a gadget's Reset button. The tip fits perfectly in the tiny hole.
+ Distinguish between medium and medium-rare steaks at a cookout. Each gets a different-colored toothpick.
+ Glue on tiny beads and sequins for an art project.
+ Mark the end of a roll of clear tape.

+ Plug a small hole in a hose. Insert the pick, snip it so it's flush with the hose, and wrap around it with electrical tape.

towel

USE TO: Keep plants hydrated. Before going away for up to a week, first thoroughly water plants. Then place a towel in a bathtub or a sink, fill with about two inches of water, and place plants on top of the towel to soak up the water gradually.
+ Support your lumbar region. Roll a towel and place it horizontally behind your lower back on a chair or a car seat.
+ Make a workout more challenging. Knot a large towel and place it between your knees (as you would a rubber ball) when doing squats.

towel rod

USE TO: Assemble a spray-cleaner arsenal. Install a rod in the utility closet or under the sink, then hook the handles onto it.
+ Keep tablecloths and linens wrinkle-free between uses. Hang them from a rod mounted to the back of the linen-closet door.

toy animals and figures

USE TO: Soothe a little one's wounds. Chill a beanbag toy animal in the freezer for use as a kid-friendly ice pack.

+ Inspire tidiness. Turn action figures into cool hooks for coats, hats, book bags, or towels. Position the arms straight out and apply a two-part epoxy over arms, shoulders, and torso, following the package directions. Mount on the wall with two screws through the torso.

toy box

USE TO: Store off-season clothing. To make the chest even more functional, give it a coat of paint and stick a store-bought seat cushion to the top with adhesive Velcro strips.

◂ transparent tape

USE TO: Seal the end of a frayed shoelace until you pick up a new pair.

+ Pluck off dry (not cracked) bits from lips before applying lipstick.

+ Enhance your flower arrangements. Apply tape in a grid across the mouth of a vase for an invisible, beginner-friendly spacing guide.

+ Reinforce the edge of a sheet of paper before using a hole punch on it.

+ Weatherproof garden seed markers.

+ Keep a plaster wall from chipping when you hang a picture. Place a small piece of tape over the spot where you plan to hammer in the nail.

+ Remove dust and crumbs from a keyboard. Slide a short strip between the letters.

+ Cover the label on a favorite lipstick so the shade name doesn't fade away.

+ Test-drive a new shade of nail polish. Place a piece of tape over a nail, then brush on a no-commitment coat.

travel-size bottles

USE TO: Lighten the load of your lunch bags. Pack single servings of salad dressing in shampoo containers.

tube socks

USE TO: Protect wood floors. Slide socks onto the legs of chairs and tables so they don't scratch the floor when you rearrange the room (yet again).

+ Sheathe shoes in a suitcase.

+ Prevent windshield wipers from freezing in place. Slip socks onto the blades on an icy evening.

turkey baster

USE TO: Change the water in a vase without disturbing the arrangement. Suction out the dirty water, then add fresh water from the tap.

+ Extract excess water from a soggy potted plant.

tutu

USE TO: Create an enchanting nightstand for a little girl's room. Wrap a tutu around a kitchen stool and secure it with staples or double-sided tape.

twist ties

USE TO: Streamline tangled cords. Secure several together or shorten a too-long cord by looping the center and wrapping it with a tie.

Twister mat

USE TO: Protect—and brighten up—the dining table during a kids' party. Right-hand red Kool-Aid spills and left-hand blueberry-pie blobs won't become permanent features.

MASTER MULTITASKER / TENNIS BALL / 1 To open a stubborn jar lid without straining, slice a ball in half, use the rubber lining to grip the lid, and twist. **2 A halved ball is also a great way to remove a warm bulb that has just burned out. 3** Add resistance to jumping jacks and lunges with weights made from tennis balls filled with pennies (about ¾ pound each). Make a small slit in a ball, insert the coins, and seal with duct tape or Super Glue. **4 Cut dryer time for a bulky comforter by tossing a few balls in with it. 5** To relieve neck tension, tie two balls in a sock, lie on the floor, and place the sock under the spot where your head and neck meet. Tuck your chin and gently nod up and down. **6 To fake out thieves, cut a slit in a ball and store valuables inside. 7** Protect floors from scratches by cutting X's in four balls and sliding them onto an ironing board's feet after their caps have come off. **8 Massage feet by putting two balls in a tube sock and rolling sore soles over them.**

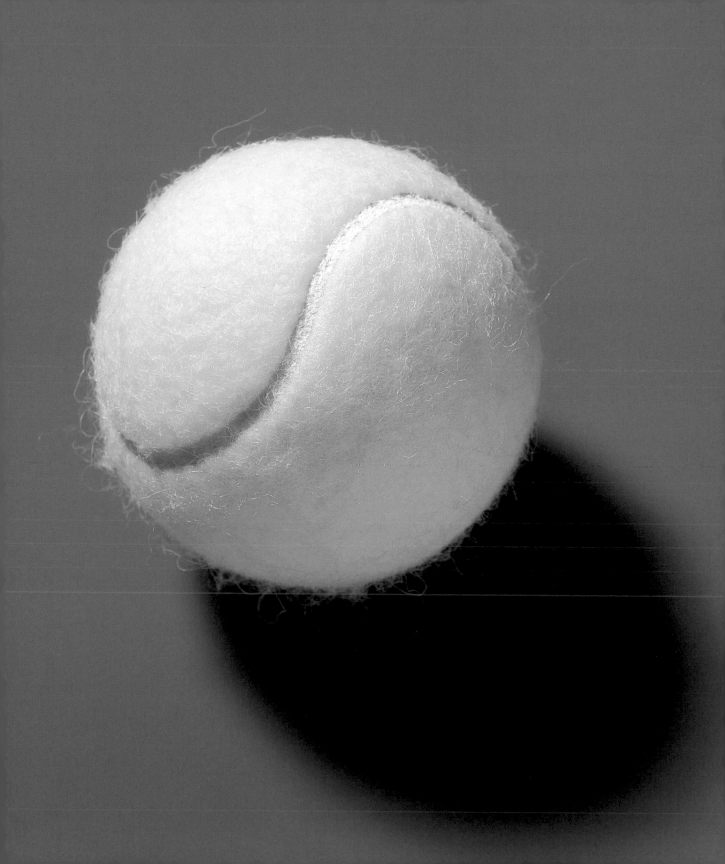

U-bolt to upholstery tacks ▶

U-bolt

USE TO: Stake a garden hose. Stagger several bolts over the length of the hose to keep it in place.

Ugg boot

USE TO: Wrangle a hot pan. Cut a square from the shaft of a boot and use it to grab hot handles. (Clean the shearling first.)
+ Cushion an uncomfortable seatbelt strap. Cut off the "leg" of the boot and slide it over the belt for a soft buffer.

umbrella ▶

USE TO: Air-dry laundry. When an umbrella has lost the capacity to fend off raindrops, cut away the fabric and hang the frame upside down from a shower rod. Clip small, light items to the ribs with clothespins.

+ Keep beach toys from rolling out to sea. Upend an open umbrella, plant its point in the sand, and use it to collect balls, Frisbees, and other objects.
+ Grow vines in the garden. Remove the fabric from a family-size umbrella and upend the spokes so they point upward. Stake it into the ground 8 to 10 inches deep. Vines such as morning glory and clematis will curl themselves along the spokes for a whimsical display.

umbrella sleeve

USE TO: Corral desk tools. Pin a sleeve to a memo board so pens can be found just where you need them.
+ Provide tech support. Fill an unneeded nylon cover with uncooked rice, stitch up the open end, and use it to cushion your wrist during marathon e-mail (or online shopping) sessions.

umbrella stand

USE TO: Contain gift-wrapping supplies. Stand rolls of paper in the center and clip bows along the rim.

+ Hold sports rackets, rods, bats, and putters.

upholstery tacks

USE TO: Dress up a cabinet or a drawer. Add tacks in a decorative pattern to the front of a piece of wooden furniture. Or help a child learn to tidy up by spelling out *socks* or *pj's* on a dresser drawer.
+ Even out a wobbly table. Hammer a round-headed tack into the bottom of a problem leg to give it a boost.
+ Add variety to a bulletin board. Mix in upholstery tacks with the pushpins.

vanilla extract to votive-candle holder ▶

vanilla extract

USE TO: Soften the smell of fresh (nonwhite) paint. Add a few drops of extract to a can.
+ Trade frostbite funk for a more pleasing scent in your freezer. Wipe it out with a cotton pad dampened with pure extract.

vase

USE TO: Serve up a cake. Flip a vase over and attach a plate on top with double-sided tape. (Use a heavy vase that won't shift when you serve.)
+ Grow herbs. Place some pebbles (for drainage) in a few vases, then plant a kitchen garden. Toss in extra soil under the roots of seedlings if needed.

+ Add personality to a shelf. Filling a clear vase with a collection of seashells, marbles, or other small objects not only increases its appeal but also gives it enough heft to stand in as a bookend.
+ Showcase a piece of coral, a signed baseball, or another trinket. Place the object on a plate and upend a clear vase over it.
+ Store rolls of toilet paper decoratively. Stack them in a tall, clear vase.
+ Tidy countertops. Gather tall kitchen tools, like spatulas and spoons, in a widemouthed vase.

vegetable bag

USE TO: Remove caked-on food from dishes. Wad the mesh into a ball, add soap and water, and scrub away.

vegetable peeler

USE TO: Churn out easy cheese curls. Run a peeler over Parmesan to create ribbons for dressing up salad, pasta, or risotto.

Velcro ▶

USE TO: Inspire your kids with housekeeping habits that will stick. To encourage them to put away their toys, affix the rough sides of a few Velcro strips to the wall, and the soft sides to the backs of stuffed animals.

+ Close gaps on a jacket or a blouse. Sew small pieces of Velcro between buttons.
+ Hang artwork. Stick a few pieces of Velcro to the back of a lightweight, glassless frame and to the wall.
+ Depill a sweater.
+ Anchor a slide-prone cushion, a small rug, a picnic-table cloth, or Fido's bowl firmly in place.
+ Put wayward cords under wraps.
+ Keep the remote from getting swallowed up by the couch. Attach Velcro to it and to the side of the TV.
+ Tack a pen conveniently by the desk calendar.

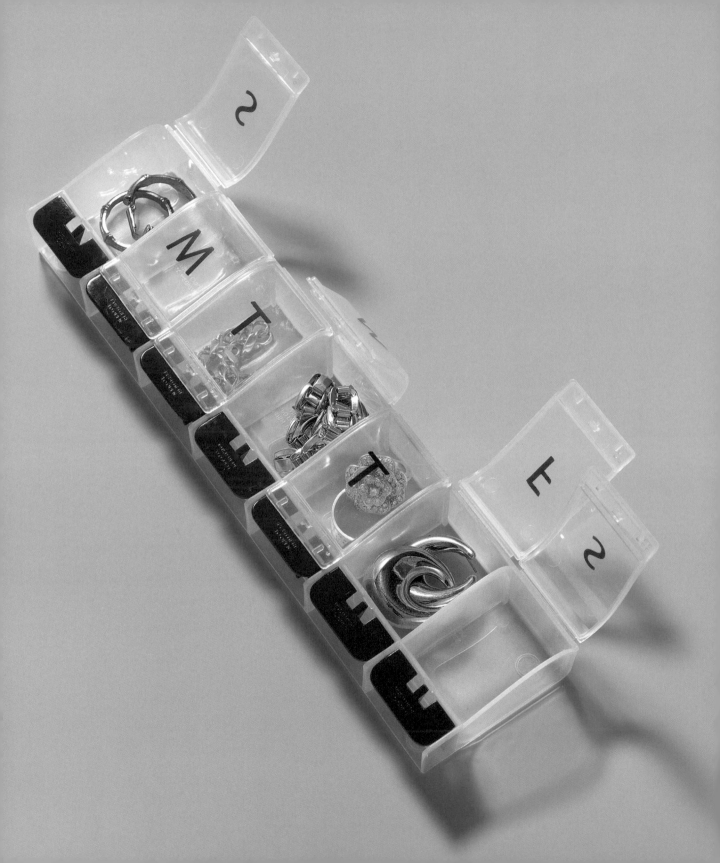

vinegar

For this Master Multitasker's many uses, see page 166.

◄ **vitamin holder**

USE TO: Hold the jewelry you need for a week away. Earrings, necklaces, and rings will travel safely and free of tangles in your suitcase or handbag.

+ Pack makeup. Slice off chunks of stick foundation, blush, and lipstick and pop them into the compartments.

+ Make an on-the-go sewing kit. Stash a thimble, extra buttons, safety pins, needles, and lengths of several colors of thread inside the cubbies.

vodka

USE TO: Restore a diamond's sparkle. Before putting the stone in a soap soak, dip them briefly in vodka to dissolve any greasy buildup.

+ Freshen musty clothes. A few sprays will kill bacteria and, when dry, won't leave a smell.

+ Loosen an adhesive bandage once a wound has healed. Dab a soaked cotton ball onto the sticky part, then peel off the bandage without pain.

+ Prevent paperwhite narcissi from going limp. Add a few drops of vodka when you water them. This will stunt their growth and keep the leaves and stems upright.

votive-candle holder

USE TO: Stylishly present toothpicks at a buffet.

+ Indulge a sweet tooth in a sensible way. Fill holders with individual portions of favorite treats, like trifle and pudding.

+ Set a luminous table. Write guests' names on strips of parchment paper and wrap them around votive holders, securing the ends with tape. Use the holders as candlelit place cards.

+ Set a snappy table. For place cards without the candles, cut a photograph of each guest to match the height of a holder, then curl it and set it inside a clear-glass holder, picture facing out.

MASTER MULTITASKER / **VINEGAR (WHITE)** / **1** To lift coffee or tea stains from a cup, swish 2 tablespoons of vinegar around, then wash. **2 In a savory recipe, ½ teaspoon vinegar can substitute for 1 teaspoon lemon juice. 3** To reduce soap buildup on a dishwasher's inner mechanisms (and thus on glassware), run the (empty) machine once a month with a cup of vinegar. **4 Paint a stubborn price sticker with several coats of vinegar, let sit for five minutes, then lift it off. 5** Erase salt stains from boots with a vinegar-dipped cloth. **6 Fluff up wool sweaters by adding a few capfuls of vinegar to the rinse cycle. 7** Kill weeds in the cracks of sidewalks or between paving stones by spraying with vinegar several times. **8 To clean a teakettle, boil vinegar and water, then wipe out grime. For a coffeemaker, put the mixture through a cycle, then run water through a few times. 9** Dab vinegar on scratched leather shoes or bags (test on a hidden spot first), let dry, then buff with colorless shoe polish.

wagon to wristwatch ▶

wagon

USE TO: Play cocktail waitress at a backyard bash. Fill the cart with ice and beverages and make the rounds once an hour, or whenever people appear to be parched.

wall calendar

USE TO: Give the art from months past new life on a present. Wrap small items, like paperback books, with the pretty pages (the ones *without* doctor's appointments and playdates scribbled on them).

wallpaper ▶

USE TO: Line drawers and shelves. Eye-catching wallpaper scraps can enliven even the infamous junk drawer.
+ Cover a schoolbook to make homework more appealing—or disguise a guilty-pleasure beach read.

walnut

USE TO: Revive hardwood floors. Rub shelled nuts into shallow scratches. Their natural oils help hide the flaws.

washing machine

USE TO: Chill drinks for a party. Fill the tub with ice and beverages so you don't have to empty the refrigerator to make room. For easy cleanup, run the spin cycle to drain the water.

water bottle

USE TO: Keep menus, playbills, maps, and other scrapbook-worthy souvenirs from bending and tearing in a suitcase. Roll them all up together, then drop them into a dry, widemouthed bottle.
+ Buy yourself extra time to get fresh flowers home un-wilted. Place the stems in a half-full plastic bottle with its top lopped off, set it in a backseat cup holder, and finish your errands.

wax paper

USE TO: Clean floors. If you run out of the regular cleaning cloths for a Swiffer-style sweeper, substitute a piece of wax paper roughly the same size. As you sweep highly trafficked and dirty areas, the gunk will stick.

WD-40

USE TO: Remove crayon marks from almost any surface (plastic, metal, TV screens, freshly painted walls). Dab on a small amount and rub away with a clean cloth.
+ Dissolve the remnants of adhesives left behind by stickers or tape.

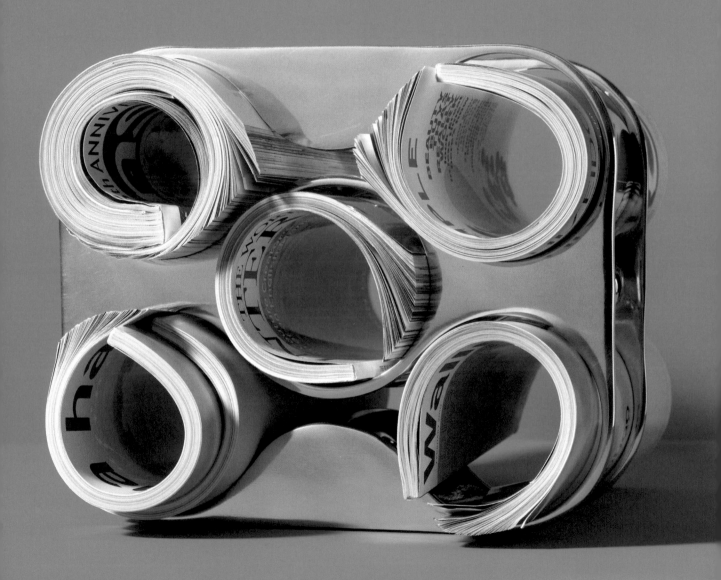

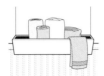

window box

USE TO: Hold towels in a guest bathroom. Roll several and place them in the box so no one has to poke around your linen closet hunting for them.
+ Show off a prized collection of trinkets. Mount the bottom of a straight-edged wooden version on the wall as a shadow box.
+ Store your CDs and DVDs.

window cleaner

USE TO: Polish your stainless-steel surfaces. Spray, then buff with a soft T-shirt.

window decal

USE TO: Decorate—and distinguish—wineglasses at a get-together. (Use small, easily removable jelly decals.)

wine bottle

USE TO: Preserve the shape of tall leather boots. Place a bottle into each shaft for reinforcement.
+ Package party favors. Send guests home with some of your special sauce or cocktail mix. Replace the labels with homemade versions if you like.

+ Roll out cookie dough or piecrust. Press down firmly on the bottle with one hand; grip the neck and steer with the other.
+ Avoid muscle strain from hefting a heavy tin of olive oil. If you buy oil by the gallon, do what they do in the Mediterranean: Pour some into a clean, dark wine bottle (light deteriorates the oil) and top it off with a pouring spout.

◄ wine rack

USE TO: File magazines. Roll up the most recent issues and slide them into the spots that are usually reserved for your favorite reserves.

wineglass

USE TO: Elevate tealights or plain votives. For romantic lighting that may go with your table decor better than those old brass candlesticks, place candles in thick-walled wineglasses. Set the candles in a thin layer of sand or small pebbles, both to anchor them and to make wax cleanup a snap.

wire hanger

For this Master Multitasker's many uses, see page 176.

wooden crate

USE TO: Store towels in the bath, T-shirts in a bedroom, or books anywhere. A single crate that once teemed with clementines or a flea-market find meant for wine bottles provides efficient storage in tight spaces. Two or more together look like furniture. Secure two stacked crates by using wood glue (and clamps) or nails between them and brackets and short screws in the back.
+ Make a toy chest or a work cart on wheels. Attach casters to a plain, stained, or painted fruit or wine crate and let the good (or at least productive) times roll.

wooden spoon

USE TO: Dry a rubber or knit glove. Slide the handle into a finger and set the spoon in a vase or a jar. This will help a knit glove keep its shape as it dries.
+ Transfer a hot, dripping, unwieldy turkey from roasting pan to carving board without the oops. Insert one sturdy spoon into each end and lift.

wrapping paper

USE TO: Create a festive, disposable table runner in minutes. Cut a sheet to the desired length from a roll and make zigzag edges with pinking shears. Secure the paper to a tablecloth or a table with pieces of double-sided tape.

+ Customize an inexpensive wall clock's face. Remove the front or back and detach the hands. Trace the outline of the face on the back of a piece of wrapping paper. Apply a spray adhesive to the original face, then affix the new one. Reassemble the clock and hang for a look that makes a statement time after time.
+ Turn plain boxes into pretty office storage. Instead of shelling out for ho-hum bins from the office-supply store, cover old shoe or computer-paper boxes with gift wrap and label them with gift tags.

wristband ▶

USE TO: Safeguard delicate pinkies from an extra-hot latte cup.

+ Cushion wine bottles. When you are bringing two or more bottles to a party or a picnic, slip a band around each one's middle as a buffer in the bag. The bands will also absorb condensation and help keep the glass from sliding through your hands.

wristwatch

USE TO: Keep track of your earrings when you hit the gym or the spa. Place studs through the holes on the strap, then attach the backs.

MASTER MULTITASKER / WIRE HANGER / 1 Use wire cutters to snip a few six-inch lengths from hangers, then bend each one into an arch to hold a soaker hose in place in a flower bed. **2 Use a hanger to fashion a wreath. The wire creates the frame you wrap with a garland. 3** Bend a hanger into a giant bubble-blowing wand, and use a solution of 1 part dish soap to 1 part water in a dishpan to make the bubbles. **4 To stop static cling, run the long side of a wire hanger over spots where clothing tends to bunch or climb. 5** To make a handy dispenser for gift-wrapping ribbon, untwist a hanger (or pop out the cardboard-tube bottom of one from the dry cleaner) and slide on the spools. Retwist (or pop the tube back in) and hang for easy storage until the next occasion arises. **6 Pull a hanger into a roughly round shape, cover it with a panty-hose leg, and use it to filter anything you wouldn't want to pass through your kitchen colander (like leafy pool water).**

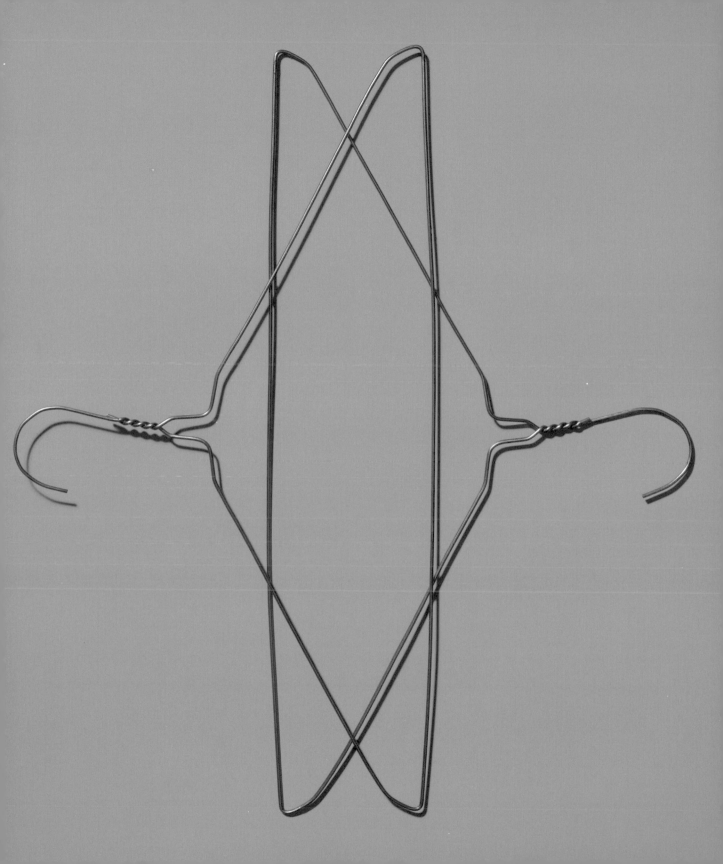

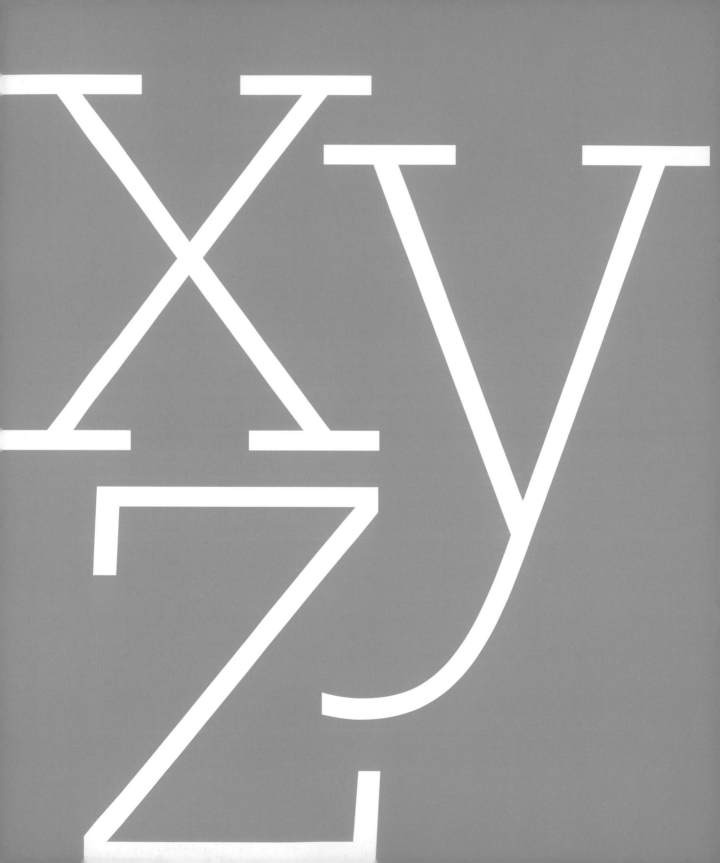

xylophone to zippered plastic bag ▶

xylophone

USE TO: Display notes for the kids. Hang an outgrown toy metal version by their door or in the family room and use magnets to tack on reminders ("Feed Buster"; "Call Grandma").
+ Compose a fun cupcake display for a child's party. Arrange treats along the keys.

yoga mat

USE TO: Line cabinets and cushion glassware. Cut the mat to fit.

+ Transport a (rolled-up) poster safely.
+ Save your seat. Cut a mat into quarters and layer them on hard (or rain-damp) stadium bleachers.
+ Collect snowy boots. Set a towel-covered mat by the door before a winter gathering.

yogurt container

USE TO: Raise a seedling. Poke drainage holes in the bottom and fill with soil to start seeds until plants are ready for pots or the garden.
+ Measure one cup of ingredients. Fill an eight-ounce container to within a pinkie's width of the rim.

zester

USE TO: Mince garlic. Remove the papery skin and rub a clove across a dishwasher-safe Microplane.

zippered plastic bag ▶

USE TO: Stockpile soup for a rainy day. Pour leftovers into labeled bags, lay them flat in the freezer, and stack when hard.
+ Cushion breakable (or crumb-prone) cargo. Slide a straw into a bag that is nearly closed and blow to inflate it. Remove the straw and finish sealing the protective bubble. (For heirlooms, play it safe with Bubble Wrap.)

+ Pipe frosting. Snip off a tiny corner to use as a pastry bag.
+ Organize panty hose. To keep hose snag-free in the drawer, store each pair in a bag with a label from the original packaging.
+ Knead dough without getting sticky fingers. Drop it into a bag, or slip a bag over your hand like a glove.
+ Remove stuck-on gum or candle wax from a tablecloth, a couch, or carpeting. Rub with a bag filled with ice cubes until the goo hardens. Shatter the gum with a blunt object, then vacuum up the chips. Carefully peel off the frozen wax with a plastic spatula.

10 new uses for this book
(Yes, the one you're holding right now.)

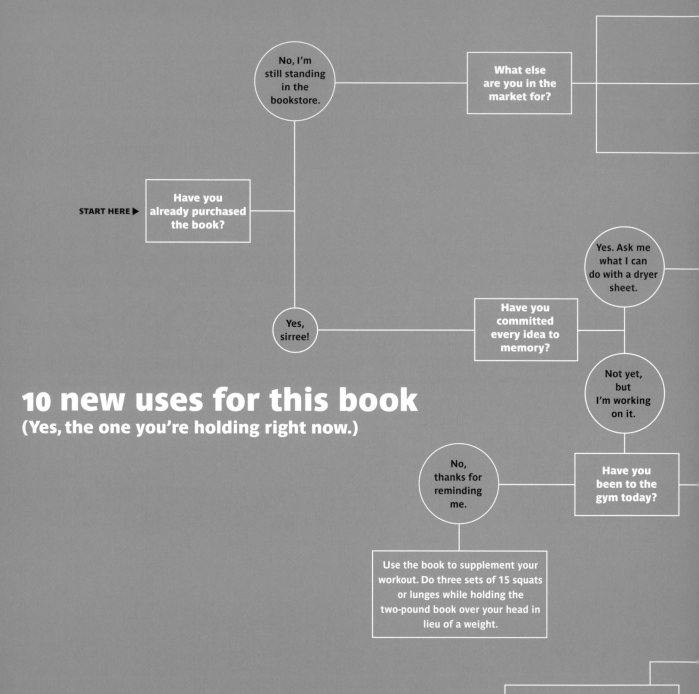

START HERE ▶

Have you already purchased the book?

No, I'm still standing in the bookstore.

What else are you in the market for?

Yes, sirree!

Have you committed every idea to memory?

Yes. Ask me what I can do with a dryer sheet.

Not yet, but I'm working on it.

Have you been to the gym today?

No, thanks for reminding me.

Use the book to supplement your workout. Do three sets of 15 squats or lunges while holding the two-pound book over your head in lieu of a weight.

Create a colorful side table. Place larger hardcovers toward the bottom of a stack and smaller books (like this one) toward the top.

self-help

trashy tabloids

Use the book to camouflage whatever else you're flipping through.

a gift for a friend

Um, hello, just slap a bow on this thing!

Let's just say they know me by name.

Use the book to organize your takeout menus. Slot them under the relevant letter (Domino's Pizza under *D*, New Moon Chinese under *N*).

How often do you order takeout?

Not lately. Someone stole all my money!

Thwart future thieves with a safe! Using an X-Acto knife, cut a square out of the middle of the book for keys, cash, and other valuables, then place on a shelf for (literal) safekeeping.

Yes, thank heaven that's over.

So what's next on your to-do list?

decorating my living room.

Organizing old photos.

Ask me again when I've logged off Facebook.

Well, then simply prop your laptop up on a long edge of the book for an ergonomic fit and more air circulation.

Use the book as a measuring device in a pinch. It's 7⅝ inches wide, 9¼ inches high, and a bit under 1 inch thick.

Place photographs with curled edges inside the book and leave them there overnight to straighten out.

Use a colorful chapter opening page as a mat in a frame that's slightly too big.

CREDITS

REAL SIMPLE

managing editor Kristin van Ogtrop
creative director Janet Froelich
executive editor Sarah Humphreys
deputy managing editor Jacklyn Monk

president, lifestyle group Steve Sachs
publisher Kevin White
vice president, consumer marketing
Carrie Goldin
**vice president, brand development and
strategy** M. Gary Ryan
vice president, marketing Sarah Kate Ellis
advertising director Melissa Gasper
public relations director Katy Reitz

TIME HOME ENTERTAINMENT

publisher Richard Fraiman
general manager Steven Sandonato
executive director, marketing services
Carol Pittard
director, retail and special sales
Tom Mifsud
director, new product development
Peter Harper
**director, bookazine development and
marketing** Laura Adam
publishing director, brand marketing
Joy Butts
assistant general counsel Helen Wan
marketing manager Victoria Alfonso
design and prepress manager
Anne-Michelle Gallero
book production manager
Susan Chodakiewicz

STAFF FOR THIS BOOK

editor Rachel Hardage
art director Eva Spring
associate editor Sharon Tanenbaum
contributing editors Candy Gianetti,
Valerie Rains
associate art director Michele Walthers
copy chief Nancy Negovetich
copy editors Pamela Grossman,
Marjorie Holt
research chief Westry Green
researcher Robin Klein
photo director Casey Tierney
associate photo editor
Lindsay Dougherty Rogers
photographer James Wojcik
photographer's assistants
Marco T. Crawford, Erica McCartney,
Bob Moyers
prop stylist Linden Elstran
prop stylist's assistant Karin Weiner
illustrator Kate Francis
custom typography designer Jeremy Mickel
editorial production director
Jeff Nesmith
editorial production manager
Albert Young
editorial production associate
Joan Weinstein
imaging director Richard Prue
imaging managers Claudio Muller,
Al Rufino
imaging specialist Bob Pizaro

SPECIAL THANKS TO

The editors and art directors—past and present—who have contributed to the New Uses for Old Things section of the magazine: Kristin Appenbrink, Amanda Armstrong, Heath Brockwell, Kelley Carter, Jamie Dannecker, Philip Ficks, Tamara Frankfort, Lindsay Funston, Pilar Guzmán, Rachel Hardage, Sarah Humphreys, Jenny Kim, Elsa Mehary, Anne-Marie O'Neill, Melinda Page, Jenny Rosenstrach, Dan Shaw, Sarah Smith, Eva Spring, Sharon Tanenbaum, Ashley Tate, Jessica Weit, Erin Whelan, Elizabeth Wells, and Ellene Wundrok. (And, of course, special thanks to their resourceful mothers, who were repeatedly contacted to share a clever use for a dryer sheet, coffee filter, zippered plastic bag—you name it.)

ACKNOWLEDGEMENTS

Christine Austin, Jeremy Biloon, Glenn Buonocore, Tracey Carl, Jim Childs, Rose Cirrincione, Jacqueline Fitzgerald, Carrie Frazier, Lauren Hall, Suzanne Janso, Brynn Joyce, Mona Li, Brian Madigan, Robert Marasco, Amy Migliaccio, Randi Mitev, Patrick O'Leary, Barry O'Meara, Kimberly Posa, Brooke Reger, Dave Rozzelle, Ilene Schreider, Adriana Tierno, Alex Voznesenskiy, Sydney Webber.

Copyright © 2010 by Time Home Entertainment Inc. Photography copyright © 2010 James Wojcik. Published by Real Simple Books, an imprint of Time Home Entertainment Inc., 135 West 50th Street, New York, NY 10020. *Real Simple* is a trademark of Time Inc.

First printing: August 2010
ISBN 10: 1-60320-140-8
ISBN 13: 978-1-60320-140-7
Library of Congress Control Number: 2010927613
Printed in China

We welcome your comments and suggestions about Real Simple Books. Please e-mail us at books@realsimple.com. If you would like to order any of our hardcover Collector's Edition books, please call us at 1-800-327-6388 (Monday through Friday, 7 A.M. to 8 P.M.).

REAL SIMPLE®

REAL SIMPLE
| LIFE MADE EASIER |

speed cleaning
FAST SOLUTIONS TO
GET THE JOB DONE.

24 BATHING SUITS FOR EVERY BODY TYPE

PROBLEM-SOLVING PRODUCTS FROM $5

JUST LIKE MOM MADE: TIME-TESTED FAMILY RECIPES

COULD DOWNSIZING IMPROVE YOUR LIFE?

Enjoy
6 FREE issues!

Discover a magazine all about making your life easier. Every issue brings you ...

- Time-saving recipes
- Quick ways to save cash
- Speed-cleaning techniques
- Effortless style and beauty
- And much more!

6 FREE ISSUES R.S.V.P.

YES! Send me 12 issues (1 year) of REAL SIMPLE — **PLUS 6 more issues absolutely FREE!** That's a total of 18 monthly issues for the special low rate of $24. If I don't enjoy the magazine, I can cancel at any time and receive a full refund on all unmailed issues.

Send for your 6 FREE issues Today!

Name _____ (Please Print)

Address _____

City _____ State _____ Zip _____

E-mail _____

☐ Payment enclosed.   ☐ Bill me later.

REAL SIMPLE

Plus sales tax where applicable. REAL SIMPLE is published monthly and may also publish occasional extra issues.
Offer good in U.S. and Canada only. In Canada, the rate is 18 issues for $34.95 plus GST, HST, and QST as applicable.
Your first issue will mail 4-8 weeks from receipt of order.

10INBIAA   005601

REAL SIMPLE

Get ready to enjoy a simpler life ...

ORGANIZING We've got clever strategies for organizing your closets, your time, and your life.

STYLE & BEAUTY Get gorgeous in 10 minutes or less, with makeup and fashion tips from the pros.

FOOD Every issue brings you dozens of quick recipes for easy weeknight meals – plus stress-free entertaining tips and more.

MONEY Discover practical ways to spend smarter, lower bills, and find the best deals online.

✂ PERE AND MAIL

FREE
ISSUES
R.S.V.P.

Send for your 6 FREE issues Today!